Seven

**Richard
Dyer**

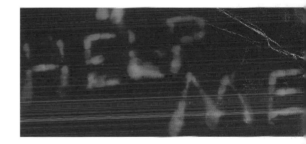

 Publishing

First published in 1999 by the
British Film Institute
21 Stephen Street, London W1P 2LN

The British Film Institute is the UK national
agency with responsibility for encouraging
the arts of film and television and conserving
them in the national interest.

Series design by Andrew Barron &
Collis Clements Associates

Typeset in Italian Garamond and Swiss 721BT
by D R Bungay Associates, Burghfield, Berks

Printed in Great Britain by
Norwich Colour Print, Drayton, Norfolk

British Library Cataloguing-in-Publication Data
A catalogue record for this book is available
from the British Library
ISBN 0-85170-723-8

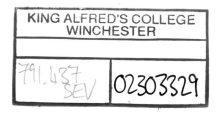

BFI Modern Classics

Rob White
Series Editor

Advancing into its second century, the cinema is now a mature art form with an established list of classics. But contemporary cinema is so subject to every shift in fashion regarding aesthetics, morals and ideas that judgments on the true worth of recent films are liable to be risky and controversial; yet they are essential if we want to know where the cinema is going and what it can achieve.

As part of the British Film Institute's commitment to the promotion and evaluation of contemporary cinema, and in conjunction with the influential BFI Film Classics series, BFI Modern Classics is a series of books devoted to individual films of recent years. Distinguished film critics, scholars and novelists explore the production and reception of their chosen films in the context of an argument about the film's importance. Insightful, considered, often impassioned, these elegant, beautifully illustrated books will set the agenda for debates about what matters in modern cinema.

Contents

to Giorgio

Acknowledgments

I should like to thank the following who have discussed aspects of *Seven* with me: Jonathan Bignell, Deborah Cameron, Christa Lykke Christensen, Gerry Cousin, Ian Garwood, Neil Jackson, Peter Kemp, Fran Lanigan and Julianne Pidduck, as well as students on my 1997–8 MA course at Warwick University, respondents to talks at the Universities of Salerno and Saragossa and the Istituto Universitario Orientale in Naples and Marina Vitale, Chantal Cornut-Gentille D'Arcy and Silvana Carotenuto, Lidia Curti and Iain Chambers, respectively, for inviting me to give those talks. Finally, I'd especially like to thank Sissel Vik, whose MA dissertation made me realise how interested I too was in the serial killer motif, Rob White, a vindication of the value of editing, and Giorgio Marini, to whose enthusiasm for the beauty of *Seven* I hope I have done justice.

1 Sin

'It's gonna go on and on and on.'
(Detective Somerset on learning of the first murder)

Seven is a study in sin. It is also a crime movie and a film of great formal rigour. The notion of sin connects these generic and stylistic qualities. Crime fiction deals by definition in matters of wrongdoing, but the specific resonance of sin is achieved in *Seven* by the single-mindedness of the film's formal – structural, aural, visual – choices.

Seven asks to be seen in terms of sin. The title need not of itself indicate this. The seven deadly sins are only one of many significant sevens in Western culture: days of Creation and of the week, cardinal virtues, Christian sacraments, wonders of the world, pillars of wisdom, colours of the rainbow; the Book of Revelation has over fifty groupings of seven (including churches, candlesticks, angels, trumpets) in its vision of the Apocalypse. Nor is this exclusively Western: the Qur'àn and the Rig-Veda are full of sevens.[1] *Seven* draws attention to more: Dante's seven terraces of purgation, a reference to seven children slain in something Detective Somerset reads. By being so starkly titled, *Seven* may want to evoke these quasi-cosmic (even New Age, *X-Files*) resonances, a vein subsequently mined in a serial killer context by the TV series *Millennium*. However, it explicitly refers only to sins and days.

The campaign for the film suggested that the former were the more important. As Chris Pula, head of marketing at the distributors New Line, put it,[2] the sins were the selling point of the film. Important as the drawing power of Brad Pitt and Morgan Freeman was, still the 'star of the movie was the crime. Brad and Morgan were the co-stars. Yes, their names were there. But we showcased the crime, the seven deadly sins.' The most widely-used poster, in turn used for the video box, exemplifies this; a TV campaign flashed the names of the sins up one by one, while a web site gave their 'more obscure details'.

This is good marketing because it understands the product. The film too insists on the primacy of sin. Its central conceit is that of the seven deadly sins used as the basis for seven murders over seven days. This is of course the killer's conceit, but it also prompts, through the Morgan Freeman character, Detective Somerset, the wider perception of human frailty evoked by the notion of sin.

Somerset is the site of wisdom in the film. This is so in two senses. First, he is the character in this detective story who is best at detection: he is the first to perceive that the first murder will be one of a series and then its pattern; he tracks the killer down by ingeniously using the public library system (following up on people who draw out apocalyptic and sadistic titles). He is painstakingly methodical, a 'great brain', as his immediate superior says. This is established by his following up on apparently irrelevant clues in the first murder: bruises on the side of the victim's head, grocery store receipts, lino strips found in the victim's stomach. These clues baffle or are brushed aside by the other detectives involved: the pathologist, the captain in charge and, most significantly, Somerset's new partner Mills (Brad Pitt). However, the importance he attaches to the clues and his interpretation are correct. In narrative terms, he is the one who knows.

His wisdom though is more than investigative acumen. It is in his whole being. He is quiet and still; he is an older man with a soft, saddened face and mellow, resigned voice; he is Morgan Freeman, Miss Daisy's chauffeur, Robin Hood's right-hand man, the Shawshank redemption. The film repeatedly cuts to him just looking on, listening, and what he sees and hears is not just clues to a sordid mystery but the world's iniquity. In a pre-credits murder investigation, he asks whether a boy saw his mother shoot his father, and the detective on duty replies irritatedly:

What kind of fucking question is that? ... It's always these questions with you. Did the kid see it? Who gives a fuck? He's dead. His wife killed him. Anything else has nothing to do with us.

But Somerset consistently sees that anything else – what it means for a child to see such violence in the family, for instance – does have to do with all of us. Again, this sets him apart from those he works with, not just this detective, but Mills with his chatter and restlessness and the cops at the library who would rather play cards than read books.

Somerset has knowledge and wisdom and thus functions as the intellectual and moral voice of the film. This makes all the more significant his relation to the killer, Jonathan Doe (Kevin Spacey). He is not like Doe but he does see the world in much the same way, and what both see is a world drenched in endless wickedness. When towards the end, Mills accuses Doe of killing innocent people, Doe delivers a speech detailing his victims' lack of innocence, concluding:

Only in a world this shitty could you even try and say these were innocent people and keep a straight face. But that's the point. We see a deadly sin on every street corner, in every house, and we tolerate it. We tolerate it because it's common, it's trivial, we tolerate it morning, noon and night.

Somerset shares this sense of the absolute pervasiveness of sin and the world's indifference to it, even though he does not use the word sin. In a conversation with the police captain, he refers to an incident 'about four blocks from here', in which a man is out walking his dog, is attacked, has his watch stolen and 'while he's lying there on the sidewalk helpless, his attacker stabs him in both eyes'; the captain shrugs it off as 'the way it's always been'. This though is Somerset's point: an act of gratuitous cruelty is met with complacency. It's really no better than the sleazy sex club owner who, asked by Mills if he likes what he does for a living, replies 'No, I don't. But that's life isn't it?' and sits back resentful and defiant. This is why Somerset felt the fear he tells Tracy of, when he heard his partner was pregnant – 'How can I bring a child into a world like this?', a world, presumably, this shitty. Later still, in a bar after the 'Lust' murder, he tells Mills, 'I just don't think I can continue to live and work in a place that embraces and nurtures apathy as if it was a virtue', the equivalent of Doe's emphasis on the toleration of sin 'morning, noon and night'.

Somerset's detective superiority and his sense of the wickedness of the world are connected. Because he can enter Doe's way of seeing the world, he understands the structure of his crimes and how to set about tracking him down. He already knows what to make of Doe's scrawling of the words 'Gluttony' and 'Greed' at the murder scenes. Familiar with the same cultural reference points as Doe, he is able to use the public library system to trace Doe to his address.

It is not just that he is erudite, but that he approaches the crime in terms of meaning, a meaning for which he has a feeling. To research the crimes, he goes to a library, and in an extended montage sequence the film cross-cuts between him contemplating works on the seven deadly sins (including Dante's *Purgatory*, Chaucer's 'Parson's Tale' and a *Dictionary of Catholicism*) and Mills at home poring over photos and reports of the scenes of the crimes. Though bound together in common endeavour, the difference is evident: Somerset seeks to grasp the sense of the murders, Mills wants direct clues to who done it. By the end of the sequence, Mills has given up and sits watching a basketball game on television, while Somerset delivers his findings to Mills's desk, findings that we subsequently realise are accurate insights into the killer's frame of reference.

In this sequence, we enter into Somerset's process of understanding more than Mills's. We see Mills looking at the material, with four shots of it clearly signalled as point-of-view shots, anchored in his baffled gaze. With Somerset, though we repeatedly have shots of him looking, we also get many more shots of the material, often dissolving from one to another and back to Somerset, the camera tracking round him in a way that does not fix the imagery so firmly in his gaze. He is mentally, but also in visual terms literally absorbed in the imagery. We also see him working on the material, photocopying it, folding the copies, making notes. All of this echoes the opening credits sequence (by Kyle Cooper), a montage of Doe's work, mainly close-ups of items, with often his hands in view turning things, using scissors, sewing pages together, writing his notebooks, the film cutting or dissolving from shot to shot. Somerset and Doe are alike: intellectual, painstaking, absorbed; and both have a consciousness of sin.

The two sequences are in many ways different, of course. We never see Doe's face, his sequence contains many more shots and, above all, the music is different. Doe's work is accompanied by the Nine Inch Nails track 'Closer', itself a mix of reworked sounds, both from musical instruments and recorded noises, a form of 'industrial rock' evoking the alienation of the city, its prominent but jerky rhythms emphasising the fragmented quality of the imagery (short takes, double exposures, off centre, scratched).[3] Somerset's study is accompanied by Bach's 'Air on a G String', the epitome of sad serenity, its smooth flow corresponding to the steady tracks, dissolves and unobtrusive cuts of the image.

The two montage sequences suggest both the affinity and difference between Somerset and Doe. The differences are clear enough. Somerset reacts to sin with sorrow, Doe with contempt; Somerset, even in the line of duty, has never killed anyone, Doe makes it his duty to kill. They have moreover a different perception of the nastiness of the world. Doe translates his into archaic categories of depravity, detailed in his sketch of the victims in response to Mills's comment on their innocence:

[handwritten annotation: Doe's murder provides atonement, cleanses sins allows them to become 'innocent victims']

An obese man, a disgusting man who could barely stand up, a man who if you saw him on the street, you'd point him out to your friends so that they could join you in mocking him, a man who, if you saw him while you were eating, you wouldn't be able to finish your meal. And after him I picked the lawyer, ... a man who dedicated his life to making money by lying with every breath he could muster to keep murderers and rapists on the street. A woman, a woman so ugly on the inside that she couldn't bear to go on living if she couldn't be beautiful on the outside. A drug dealer, a drug dealing pederast, actually. And let's not forget the disease-spreading whore.

[handwritten annotations in right margin: paradox that he is aware of...; his angry reaction]

[handwritten annotation: surely the sin of lust was the Johns']

Doe is mobilising widespread views, or rather, where you don't share them, prejudices: against fatness, legal shenanigans, rape, murder, narcissism, drug dealing, paedophilia, prostitution. It is a rant. Of the wrongs he assembles in the speech, he does not in fact take vengeance on those most commonly now held to be wrongs: rape, murder and paedophilia.[4] Equally, the sins he actually identifies by the acts of murder are now widely considered either mere faults – Gluttony is greediness,

Sloth laziness – or even on the way to being virtues – Greed is ambition, Lust and Envy desire (which we should not repress), Wrath anger (which we should learn to express) and Pride pride. In contrast, what Somerset identifies as wickedness is violence, cruelty and indifference to them.

Yet Somerset's and Doe's are really only different ways of organising the deeper perception of a world beyond hope. When Somerset is on his way to the library in a cab, we see from his point of view a shot of random squalor and violence in the ceaseless dreary rain outside; the driver asks him where he is going and he replies, 'far away from here'; the film then cuts to a long-held shot of him looking out of the cab, a doleful face, eyes full with the pitiable vileness of the world.

I have avoided using the word evil, for I want to make here a distinction between sin and evil, one not given by the words themselves. By evil I mean the notion of a malevolent force outside of human beings, though capable of possessing them; by sin, I mean the notion of badness being constitutive of humanity and the world we have made. In the most radical, and heretical, view of sin, there is, as the *Book of Common Prayer* has it, 'no health in us' – only God's mercy can save us from ourselves and damnation. A theology of sin does recognise distinctions between degrees of wrongdoing, in particular between 'venial' and 'mortal' sin, but they are all part of the same stuff of iniquity of which humanity is ineluctably composed. It may be worse to kill than to be unkind, to torture than to fornicate, but they are all manifestations of the same propensity to wickedness.

The notion of evil, rather than sin, is a common way of dealing with serial killers, often in a context where all other explanations seem to fall short. This is equally true of the coverage of famous cases and in fictions, as at the end of *Halloween* (1978) where the psychiatrist admits that there is no explanation for the remorseless killer Michael other than that he is evil incarnate. Somerset himself invokes the notion, when he says that, if, when they finally get the killer, he turns out to be 'Satan himself', that would be satisfying. However, he goes on to say that the sad fact is 'he's not the devil, he's just a man', not an embodiment of the

otherness and exteriority of evil, but of the common fact of sin. This is
how both Somerset and Doe see the world and also how *Seven* conveys
it, the remorseless pervasiveness of shitty iniquity carried in every aspect,

Somerset's work, Mills's work, Doe's work

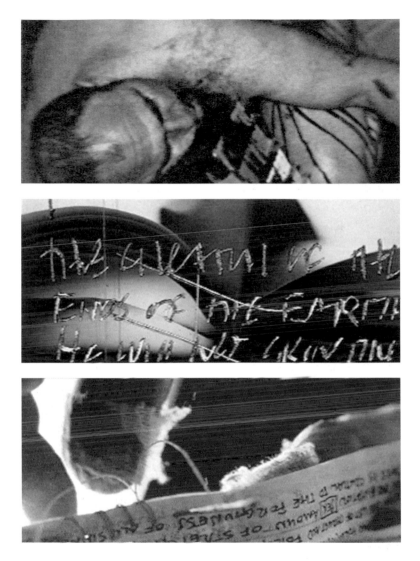

including literal darkness, grimly brooding music and the sense of incessant noise. Doe gives all this a religious gloss, whereas Somerset's is a humanist despair – but the feeling is not so different.

One of the strongest reactions I had the first two times I saw the film was a tremendous sense of the danger in which Somerset and Mills found themselves. At one level, this seems like a misreaction. When investigating the scenes of the crime, the detectives are in an obvious sense perfectly safe, apart from the one moment of danger in Mills's chase of Doe. It is partly the darkness and 'dread-full' score that convey the overriding sense of danger, and it is appropriate that they should. Mills, as the denouement reveals, is in literal danger – of death and of sin; and beyond this, in *Seven* everyone, including the audience, is in danger, because no-one is beyond the on and on and on of sin.

2 Story

In an unidentified US city, a serial killer begins a seven-day sequence of seven murders, in which each victim is identified by the killer as guilty of one of the seven deadly sins and killed appropriately (see chart). A detective due to retire in seven days, William Somerset, and a newly arrived younger detective, David Mills, are assigned to the case. Their

DAY	SIN	VICTIM	METHOD OF KILLING	NAMING THE SIN
Monday	Gluttony	'the Fat Boy'	forced to eat until his stomach bursts	written in grease behind fridge
Tuesday	Greed	Eli Gould (a defence attorney)	bleeds to death after cutting off a pound of his own flesh	written in blood on floor
Wednesday	Sloth	Victor (real name Theodore Allen)	tied to a bed for a year until expires	written in black on wall
Thursday				
Friday				
Saturday	Lust	'a hooker' (female, blonde)	fucked to death by a serrated dildo strapped onto a punter	scratched on door to sex club room
Sunday				
a.m.	Pride	unnamed beautiful woman	killer cuts off victim's face, then offers her a choice between calling for help and living disfigured or taking sleeping pills; she chooses latter	written on wall above photo of victim
7 p.m.	Envy	Jonathan Doe	shot by Mills	Doe: 'Because I envy your normal life, it seems that envy is my sin.'
7 p.m	Wrath	Detective Mills		Doe: 'Become vengeance, David. Become ... wrath.'

initial antagonism becomes respect and even affection, partly through the intervention of Mills's wife, Tracy.[5] She confides in Somerset that she is pregnant, telling him she has not told Mills because she is not sure that

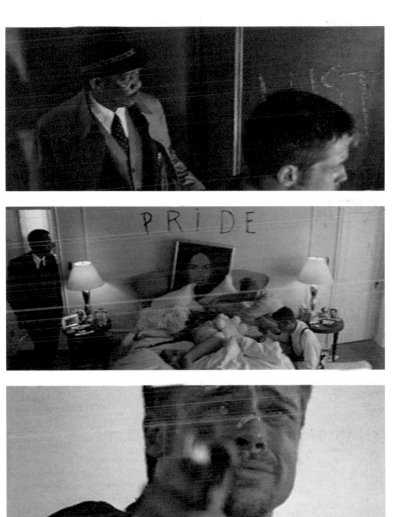

she wants to have a baby in the conditions of city life. At the scene of the 'Greed' murder, Somerset and Mills find fingerprints spelling out the words 'Help Me'; the prints are identified as belonging to one Theodore

Allen aka Victor. With a battery of police, they storm his apartment, only to find him virtually dead, the 'Sloth' victim; the killer had severed off Victor's hand to make the fingerprints. At the scene of the crime, a news photographer intrudes and Mills sends him away abusively. Somerset uses the public library system to track down the names of people with the same obsessions as the killer and this leads them to the apartment of a Jonathan Doe. The latter arrives, sees them at the door and shoots at them; they give chase and Mills ends up with Doe's gun pressed against his head, but Doe lets him go. Somerset and Mills explore the apartment and find, among other evidence that Doe is the killer, the photograph that he took of Mills when, they realise, he was posing as a press photographer at the 'Sloth' murder. Two more murders follow, and then Doe gives himself up. He says that he will not plead insanity if Somerset and Mills, and only they, will go with him to find the remaining two bodies. This is agreed. Doe directs them to a deserted area far from the city. A van arrives, delivering a box for Mills. Somerset opens it and sees that it contains Tracy's severed head. Doe tells Mills that he tried to rape Tracy, but failed and, envious of Mills's happy normality, cut off her head; in doing so, he reveals that he also destroyed the baby that Mills still did not know she was carrying; as Doe plans, Mills kills him in his Wrath, thus also effectively destroying himself.

3 Structure

'This is beginning.'
(Somerset on learning of first murder)
'He's not finished.'
(Somerset when Doe turns himself in after five murders)

Andrew Kevin Walker's original script for *Seven* contained the backbone of the film: the conceit of the seven deadly sins murders and the two *coups de théâtre*: the killer's surrender and the final murders. Yet the latter were resisted by the studios. David Fincher was sent the original script in error; the studio had wanted one climaxing in a race to save Tracy from Doe's attempt to kill her.[6] Even during shooting, pressure was exerted to change the ending, having Mills's dog's head in the box, for instance, and Somerset coldly shooting Doe. It was probably only the insistence of the person with most box office clout, Brad Pitt, an insistence written into his contract, that ensured the original ending's survival. As Pitt remarks,[7] it is 'everything [the film has] been leading up to'.

The story structure is insistently clear: seven murders in seven days in a film called *Seven* (with the numeral inserted into the title on the credits and in much publicity: *Se7en*). It is elegantly economical. It takes three standard narrative character functions: a pretext (the murder victims), a perpetrator to be investigated (the killer) and someone to do the investigating (the cops); and it then fuses them when investigated and investigator both become pretexts, and at each other hands. The victims are pretexts in two senses: they are victims before the film text reveals them as such (pre-texts) and they are the occasion for there being a story, an investigation, a text at all; however, when investigated and investigator become pretexts, they are victims whose deaths do not need investigation and thus they prevent rather than occasion any more narrative. No story's closure could be more tight.

The rigour of the structure permits internal play. When Doe has his gun at Mills's head, it is a reversal of the cop–criminal relation that is common enough at the mid-point of a thriller. However, Doe chooses not to kill Mills and runs off; Mills neither saves himself nor is saved by Somerset. This moment points backwards, to Mills telling Somerset that the first time he went out to arrest a suspect, he killed someone unnecessarily; in other words, the cop became the killer. In the Doe's-gun-at-Mills's-head encounter, on the other hand, it is the killer who acts as a cop should, who chooses not to kill unnecessarily. The moment also points forwards to the end of the film, where the situation is reversed – Mills has his gun to Doe's head and chooses to kill, even though Doe poses no physical threat to him; Doe here goads the cop into becoming the killer where before Doe the killer acted the cop.

A different kind of play occurs near the end of the film, out by the pylons where Doe has led Somerset and Mills. Doe asks the time. Somerset tells him it's 7.01 and he replies, 'It's close.' This has at least three implications. It reminds us that we are at the seventh hour of the seventh day, or rather just past it, so that Spacey can give Doe's remark a sort of ruefulness – the temporal sequencing of the murders is not quite perfect, but near enough. Secondly, it indicates that what's going to happen is on the point of happening, screwing the suspense up one notch more. Thirdly, though, it could mean that the corpses, what they have come to find, are near. This is what Mills assumes it means and he suggests they take a look; Doe leads the way, taking both of them further away from Somerset and the possibility of his restraining hand spoiling the denouement. Wittily, Doe's three words play on Mills's obtuseness and impatience, while simultaneously referring to both the film's pattern (the completion of the murder sequence) and its suspensefulness (it's about to happen).

The most important play comes, however, from the way the narrative structure is set against the background of the film's world. Within itself no structure could be more closed off: the disruption caused by the crimes has been resolved with terrible finality. In classic crime fiction this means that order and security have been restored to the world, a demonstration that such restoration is always possible. Yet the whole construction of *Seven*, above all its unending gloom and murmur, suggests that such rigorous closure has made no difference whatsoever to a world that was never ordered and secure in the first place.

It is because *Seven*'s central conceit is so strongly marked that it can permit such ironies of repetition, reversal and completion. The elegant clarity of the structure might however seem thin and dry, mere cleverness, were it not thickened in the treatment. Here I look at four elements of this: pacing, the central cop/buddy relationship, the preparation of the ending and the handling of our investment in detective stories.

The revelation of the structure would become boring if it were unfolded at an unvarying pace. Much of the actual variation is due to direction, editing, music and so on, but it is also in the structure. The set-piece of the police storming Victor's apartment is a *tour de force* of cinema, but it also comes at the right moment. The pattern of killings and the somewhat fruitless laboriousness of investigation are in danger of feeling routine. Suddenly the cops believe they have found the killer and there is an explosion of activity, inaugurated by a dynamic cut on the chief turning and walking towards a camera that backs speedily away from him as he rattles off Victor's profile. By having the police think the clues at the Greed murder point to the killer, the script provides an occasion for noise, energy, excitement. At the same time, it also provides an enigma – anyone in the audience will know they can't possibly be going to get the killer yet because it's too early in the film, so how is it going to turn out? This enigma is solved, when we realise that Victor is in fact the next victim, not the killer, and this lets the pressure down, only for the film to deliver its biggest moment of shock horror, when Victor suddenly jerks to life as the cops bend over him. Scott Reynolds, director of the serial killer movie *The Ugly* (1997), bears witness to the effect of this moment:

When the victim whose sin was sloth turned out to be alive, I nearly screamed. The hairs stood up on the back of my neck, and I felt thrilled that a film could still have that effect on me.[8]

Mills's extended chase of Doe similarly comes as a burst of invigorating speed after a period of grim waiting.

Later, the film seems to comment on the problem of pace. When, informing the police by phone of the Pride murder, Doe says, 'I've gone and done it again,' it's partly a sly mockery of conventional wisdom about serial killers (see Chapter 4, 'Seriality') but also an indication of the problem of flagging interest – here's yet another murder, bore, bore. The danger of flagging is almost at once removed by having Doe give himself up, making us wonder once again what on earth the film can do now.

The cop/buddy relationship between Somerset and Mills is at base one that has become familiar from a number of films,[9] including *Deadly Pursuit* (1988; starring Sidney Poitier and Tom Berenger), the *Die Hard* films (1988/90/92; Reginald Veljohnson/Samuel L. Jackson and Bruce Willis),[10] and especially the *Lethal Weapon* series (1987/89/95/98; Danny Glover and Mel Gibson), in the third of which the Glover character has eight days left before retirement, only one more than Somerset. The set-up – older, orderly black cop and younger, volatile white one; initial hostility developing into buddiness – was, when it first appeared, a reversal of stereotypes: in Western tradition, it is black men who are irrational and uncontrolled and white men their opposite. However, by the time of *Seven*, this reversal had become almost the norm.

Seven is not, nor was ever intended to be, part of this cycle. Fincher's initial response to the first pages of the screenplay was disinterest because he considered it 'just another buddy movie', and the producers did not like his insistence on casting Morgan Freeman (after Brad Pitt had been secured) because it might 'make it look like we were trying to ape *Lethal Weapon* in some way'. Fincher commented that he was 'kind of shell-shocked' that this was even a concern.[11] Nevertheless, *Seven*'s treatment of its central cop duo does play effectively against the cycle. In some ways it is a rejection of it. *Seven* is, for instance, short on action sequences and almost barren of wisecracking humour and the joys of virile sparring. Indeed, Mills's jokes are intrusive and inappropriate, while Somerset's occasional humour is dry as a bone and not part of by-play with Mills. Moreover, though their gradual liking of each other is touchingly sketched, their relationship, always eclipsed by the detail and horror of what they are dealing with, is never the heart of the film.

Yet *Seven* may also be seen as the apotheosis of the *Lethal Weapon* line. I will discuss later the significance of locating wisdom in the black character. Here I focus on the character of Mills. It is sometimes forgotten that the eponymous 'lethal weapon' of at least the first of the Glover–Gibson films is the Gibson character, Martin Riggs, himself. He is a Vietnam veteran, regularly a sign of likely instability in Hollywood, and at the start of the film, he has just lost his lover; he is seen by everyone as unhinged, a loose cannon who might go off, lethally. Of course, the point is that in the end he can handle himself, his recklessness does pay off or he is saved by Roger Murtaugh (Glover) (and he knows he can bank on this). The subsequent films lighten further the disturbing quality of the character, but still he is constantly endangering both his and Murtaugh's life and the success of their investigation: the elation is in his getting away with it. Mills has a similar volatility, a short fuse, a readiness to cut procedural corners, but he does not get away with it. His abuse of an intruding photographer, in fact Doe in disguise, puts Doe's back up and leads to his own death. Doe is able to use Mills's quick temper, his incipient violence, against him. Doe, as it were, realises the actual, not just titular, potential lethality of the Berenger–Willis–Gibson hero.

The encounter with Doe-as-photographer prepares the denouement, Mills's demise. Indeed, it must give Doe the idea, for at that point he cannot already know what Mills is like. We do, however. The film paints in his 'sin' through an accumulation of details: his cocky dismissal of Somerset's suggestion that they get to know each other; his impatience with Somerset's researches ('Fuckin' Dante! Goddamm poetry-writing faggot piece of shit! Fuck 'im'); his inability to laugh along whole-heartedly, ruefully, against himself, with Tracy and Somerset, when the latter jokes about the extreme effect of a train passing the Mills's apartment; the fact that, as he tells Somerset, the first time he went out on a raid of a suspect's home, he killed someone needlessly; his breaking down Doe's apartment door in a rage, even though this renders the investigation illegal. This is heightened by Brad Pitt's performance style: scratching his head, staccato jabs in the air with splayed fingers, inappropriate sniggering, the endless restlessness of incipient violence. In the car on the way to the final two murders, Doe observes that he knows that Mills would 'enjoy a time alone with me in a room without windows … it's in those eyes of yours' and as the journey proceeds Mills gets more and more angry, shouting, jabbing his finger at him, insulting him ('Sit back, you fuckin' freak! Shut your fuckin' mouth!'), in short, corroborating Doe's perception that he has found the right embodiment of Wrath.

The build-up to Mills's death is also suggested in the editing in this sequence. Mills and Somerset sit in the front, Somerset driving, with Doe in the back separated from them by a grille. Throughout, Somerset is shot from his right as if from within the car, often in extreme close-up, sometimes further back. The set-ups for Mills and Doe are more varied. The first shot of Doe in the sequence shows him reflected in the driving mirror, triply contained by the frame of the mirror, the bars of the grille and the fact that this puts him in Somerset's sights. Most other shots show him through the grille (though not always in the driving mirror); a few near the beginning of the sequence are shot as if from within the back of the car. Mills is shot as if from within the car, often across an out-of-focus Somerset in the foreground. However, he is also shot through the grille.

The commonest editing pattern cuts between Mills and Doe taunting each other and Somerset looking and listening on. The cuts between Mills and Doe usually show both of them behind bars, suggesting a connection between them, that is both an anticipation of the denouement (both will be destroyed for their sin) and an implication of their similarity. This is proposed by Doe verbally, when he admits that he enjoyed committing the murders just as Mills would enjoy 'a time alone with me in a room without windows', in other words that Mills, like him, has a pleasure in violence put to righteous ends. The consequent similarity is that they are both trapped by this; they are both behind bars.

Cuts are sometimes even more precisely and intricately linked to the dialogue and characters. Consider the following early sequence of shots:

Mills: 'We're not just going to pick up two more dead bodies, are we John? That wouldn't be shocking enough,	Mills screen left, leaning back over his left shoulder to speak to Doe; Somerset visible in profile extreme right
we've got newspapers to think about, yeah?' Doe: 'Wanting people to listen, you can't just	Doe looking straight ahead until 'yeah', on which he pauses, turns with a pained expression to Mills, turns back before speaking, but glances towards Mills on a minuscule pause before 'tap'
tap them on the shoulder anymore, the back of the car; his eyes move	Mills seen through the grille as from from Doe to Somerset
you have to hit them with a sledgehammer.'	Somerset in profile, very close-up, looking towards Mills

Mills taunts Doe with a characteristic cliché about serial killers (that they are attention-seekers); Doe starts to reply and on his glance before 'tap' the film cuts back to Mills. The cut is motivated by Doe's look and word, acting like a tap on Mills's shoulder. The editing and pronouncement reinforce each other, for if Doe is tapping on Mills's shoulder to tell him something, it is in the context of saying that 'people', of whom Mills is typical, don't pay any attention to a tap. The cut also links one of the few shots of Doe seen not through the grille to the first of those showing Mills who is, suggestive of Doe's power to condemn and destroy Mills. As Doe goes on to speak of the need for 'a sledgehammer' to get his point home, the film cuts to Somerset, apparently looking at Mills. The cut is to the character who does pay attention in the film; his look presages the implications for Mills of not paying attention.

Or consider this yet more subliminal association of shots and words:

Doe: 'Allowing five innocent people to	Somerset listening
die, until you felt like springing your	Doe seen in the driver's mirror, somewhat smaller and higher in the frame than previously
trap? Tell me, what was the indisputable evidence	Mills listening, turned looking towards Doe
that you were going to use on me ....?'	Somerset listening

Doe is responding to Mills's claim that they would have got him
'eventually', pointing out that they were not making a good job of it ('So
what were you doing? Biding your time? Toying with me? Allowing

five …'). The cut on 'die' is a cut from Somerset listening to Doe
himself, who is going to die and does not consider himself innocent. The
framing here reduces further the space Doe occupies, makes even more
apparent that this is within Somerset's sights; though Doe is in charge of
events, he is also trapped in them. The cut on 'trap' is a cut to Mills,
prefiguring the trap Doe has laid for him. 'Evidence' cuts back to
Somerset, the one person who has been able to read the evidence,
although even he has not the evidence to predict what will happen. Each
of these cuts is like an anticipatory trace of the end (Doe's death, Mills's
trap, Somerset's knowledge), but only a trace.

The ground is equally well laid in relation to Tracy. She is a crucial
character, an emblem of the possibility of virtue in the world (see
Chapter 7, 'Salvation'), yet she appears only a few times in the film and
only really reveals herself in scenes with Somerset alone, not with Mills,
her husband. We must not forget her or lose a sense of her importance
for Mills, but we must not be reminded too insistently of it, otherwise we
will too easily guess her involvement in the denouement. Only
retrospectively must we realise that the blood on Doe's hands when he
gives himself up must be hers. After her last appearance (when Mills gets
home late, cuddles up to her in bed, tells her he loves her 'so much' and
she says sleepily, 'I know'), she is frequently referred to, but in ways that
seem utterly inconsequential, just the naturalistic noise of everyday life:
as Mills goes into the police station on the last day, a woman cop hands

Tracy in the home

him a note saying his wife called and will he get his own answering
service, but he just puts it in his pocket and carries on talking to
Somerset; when discussing Doe's plea bargaining, Mills says, 'We've got
him. ... He's gonna get his free cable TV. Tell him my wife doesn't even
have cable'; getting ready to go in the car with Doe, Mills jokes with
Somerset, 'I keep coming home late, my wife's gonna think something's
up!' I am drawing attention to these remarks here, but they are so
unstressed and apparently unimportant, that they are virtually subliminal.
They remind us of Tracy even while also allowing us not think about her.
They are equivalent to the literally subliminal shot of her that flashes up
just before Mills kills Doe. She represents, archetypally, what it, policing,
the male encounter with the world, is all for; her death must be utterly
devastating, but the shock of it also depends on hiding reminders of her
in the inconsequentialities of naturalistic dialogue.

When the end comes, it feels inevitable, although I certainly never
anticipated it when I first saw the film.[12] Some people have said to me
that they could see it coming a mile off, though this usually means they
knew what was in the box. It may be that the film errs in building up the
tension around the box, such that for some viewers guessing what is in it
(and guessing correctly too easily) eclipses the more significant, and less
predictable, mutual destruction of Doe and Mills. In the details given
above, it seems to me that the film both fully prepares, justifies and

Mills's subliminal memory of Tracy

makes meaningful all three 'deaths' (Tracy, Doe and Mills), while simultaneously concealing them within the patina of everyday dialogue and interaction, and apparently purely functional editing, thus ensuring the satisfaction of an intense surprise that instantly appears inevitable, the shock of the retrospectively obvious.

The thickening of the structure makes it less stark and allows it to function effectively in terms of suspense and shock. In other words, the film works just as well in the unfolding of the story as we watch it as in the revelation of an overall pattern to the story that is fully realised by the end. All storytelling involves this combination of levels, though it is more unusual to make the pattern so apparent so early on. It is the fact of pattern, the seven deadly sins conceit, that is evident, yet we don't know what the overall pattern of the film will turn out to be. It could just be seven murders and then the killer is apprehended and brought to justice, but that would be straightforward to the point of dull; it could be four or five murders and then the cops get him, but then the pattern promised by the conceit would never be completed. We want to know and see the pattern, and the film in turn knows that we do.

Our desire to know is sinful. In a film as full of religious allusions as this, it is perhaps reasonable to point out that the foundational sin of humanity, in the Judaeo-Christian tradition, is the desire to eat of the tree of the *knowledge* of good and evil in the Garden of Eden. Even if such an allusion is not being mobilised, *Seven* certainly draws on an awareness of how much watching thrillers is about knowing – detecting but also seeing – nasty things. Hitchcock's cinema famously plays on this, teasing the viewer into a self-consciousness about the pleasure of knowing the horrible. Consider just the first and last of his serial killer movies. *The Lodger* (1926) opens with and returns repeatedly to the show 'Golden Curls', a revue with blonde chorines, at the same time establishing that the Jack the Ripper figure at large in the city prefers blondes; we are invited to get off on exactly the spectacle that incites the killer. *Frenzy* (1972) is crueller on us. One of the first murders is shown in all its horribleness. Later the killer is clearly off to perform another; the camera tracks up the stairs with him before he goes into the room, but then the door shuts in our face and the camera tracks all the way back down the stairs. The track up seems to promise us that we are going to see nastiness again; the track back, in its formal flamboyance, seems to rap us over the knuckles for having wanted to.

However, apart from *Seven* itself, the most devastating play on the viewer's desire to know in a serial killer context is *Spoorloos* (*The Vanishing*, Netherlands/France 1988), whose French title is *L'Homme qui voulait savoir* ('The Man Who Wanted to Know'). Here a young man's girlfriend is abducted while they are on holiday together; the crime goes unsolved and the young man remains obsessed with it; eventually he meets the abductor, who tells him he will let him know exactly what happened to his girlfriend, but that he must allow him to drug him so that he can take him to the place under the cloak of secrecy; when the young man wakes up he finds that – like the girlfriend – he has been buried alive; end of film. The protagonist is desperate to know; he takes the most absurd risk in the pursuit of knowledge and his curiosity is satisfied, but in the process he winds up in the most phantasmagorically final of situations. The effect of the film turns on our wanting him to take up the offer, because we want to know too, and our being punished by an ending that keeps you awake at night.

Seven plays on the same desire to know. Two-thirds of the way through John Doe gives himself up. It is devastating, since logic dictates this should be the end of the film and what could be more disappointing than that, with two murders still to go? David Fincher recalls reading the original script:

The icing on the cake was when John Doe … gives himself up. I was holding the script so I knew how many pages were left in the movie and I thought, 'Holy shit, if I'm sitting in a theatre, this movie could go on for another hour, this could be the middle of the movie'. It made me very uncomfortable.[13]

The discomfort derives from wanting the film to go on. The pattern of seven killings has been so vividly established that we want it to be completed and we want to know how it can be if the killer has now given himself up. The film assuages our discomfort only by playing still more on our desire to know.

Doe says he will take Somerset and Mills to the other bodies. Sense dictates that they should reject his offer: they have all the evidence they need, plea bargaining is morally dubious and this one's on record, and, even if Doe pleads insanity at his trial and this is accepted (itself a big if), he'll still be locked up for ever. The police go through these arguments. The lawyer puts a counter that carries some but not conclusive weight (that people will think poorly of the police if they've turned down the opportunity of uncovering two more murder victims). The decisive moment is when Mills says to Somerset, and to our relief, 'Let's finish it.' We want to know because, as Doe says to Mills in the ride to the final murders, he (Mills), which is to say we, 'can't see the whole complete act yet'. However, the – our, their – will to know is lethal. The fulfilment of the film's structure is the consummation of deadly desire.

SEVEN | 35

4 Seriality

'I've gone and done it again.'
(Doe on the phone to police headquarters *re* the Pride murder)

When John Doe sends Somerset, Mills and a phalanx of cops to Victor's apartment, he is manipulating standard views of the archetypal serial killer.[14] First, the message they discover, 'Help me,' written in bloody fingerprints at the scene of the Greed murder, uses the idea that serial killers are frequently calling for help, that they want to be caught before they commit any more murders. (In 1945 killer William Heirens scrawled in lipstick on a bedroom wall, 'For heavens sake catch me before I kill more I cannot control myself' (*sic*), a line quoted in *While the City Sleeps* (1956); in *The Sniper* (1952), the killer sends the police a note reading 'Stop Me! Find me and stop me! I'm going to do it again'; Dennis Nilsen is said to have said 'Thank God you've come' to the police when they came to arrest him in 1983.) Then, when the police identify Victor, that is, Theodore Allen, from the fingerprints, they find they have something like an FBI profile of the serial killer. The police chief briefs the cops: Allen/Victor had a strict Christian fundamentalist upbringing (evoking the widespread psycho-analytic model of the repression in childhood of natural instincts that later come out in destructive forms); he has a history of mental illness and petty crime; he is sexually perverted (he attempted rape of a minor). Though Somerset is unconvinced, Doe correctly surmises that the police will fall into assuming they've got the killer, because Victor's history coincides so neatly with this identikit profile.

Somerset's misgivings are significant. Doe is not like Victor, at any rate as far as we or the police ever find out. Though he speaks the Christian language of sin and has crucifixes in his bedroom, there is no evidence of his killing being a return of what a fundamentalist upbringing had repressed. He is not certified insane, does not have a criminal record and there is no indication that the murders are performed for sexual gratification. Nor does Doe conform to other recurrent elements in serial killer profiling: he is not so far as we know a

pr⟨⟩ ⟨⟩f childhood abuse and family break-up; his killing is not facilitated by his being nomadic.

The play with Victor is one of several points at which Doe cites the image of the typical serial killer. He tells Mills on the phone (during the investigation of his apartment) how much he admires him and 'you law enforcement agents', something reiterated by his lawyer during the bargaining that leads to the final journey. This recalls Ed Kemper's well-known admiration for the police, even to the point of befriending and hanging out with those on his case.[15] Doe buys the dildo for the Lust murder from 'Wild Bill's Leather', a name that is an amalgamation of two fictional serial killers, Buffalo Bill in *The Silence of the Lambs* (1991) and Leatherface in *The Texas Chainsaw Massacre* (1974), both of whom in turn are based on the real-life killer, Ed Gein. Doe however is not like Buffalo Bill, Leatherface or Gein and he does not use the dildo himself but gets a punter to do so. His ironically rhythmic delivery in the phone call *re* the Pride murder ('I've gone/and done it/again') evokes the notions of both confession and compulsion in serial killer discourse. In all cases, the citation seems to distance Doe from the common construction of the serial killer: his admiration seems just a trick to lure Mills, he is not an Ed Gein derivation, he mocks confession and compulsion.

However, Doe does, somewhat startlingly, fit rather exactly one of the first serial killer profiles ever made, Dr Thomas Bond's 1888 report on Jack the Ripper:

The murderer in external appearance is quite likely to be a quiet inoffensive looking man probably middle-aged and neatly and respectably dressed. ... He would be solitary and eccentric in his habits, also he is most likely to be a man without regular occupation, but with some small income or pension.[16]

This is of course an imagination of the killer, since 'Jack' has never been definitively identified, let alone caught. But it sketches an idea of the serial killer that is part of the repertoire and to which Doe belongs. In other words, while he is no Victor or Gein, he is representative of certain aspects of serial killing.

Actual serial killing is a statistically unimportant phenomenon. In the USA, much less than 1 per cent of all murders are serial murders, and so murder accounts for less than 1 per cent of all causes of death. Yet the serial killer has become a widespread figure in films, novels, television series, true crime coverage and even painting, poetry, opera and rock music. Serial killing provides a sure-fire formula for gripping storytelling, but this alone does not account for its success. The serial killer is also meaningful. Judith Walkowitz[17] notes that the Jack the Ripper murders were assumed from the start of press coverage to be somehow symptomatic of the state of things. The serial killer is assumed to be a phenomenon of modern (that is, since Jack the Ripper) and advanced societies (above all, the USA). Because serial killers are also overwhelmingly male, they have increasingly been seen to be expressive specifically of masculinity in contemporary society. Within this broad compass the serial killer may be made to be representative of a wide range of fears, intuitions, prejudices and perceptions. The fact that Doe does not fit all aspects of this representational range does not mean that he does not fit any. Here I look at those that he does articulate: he is male, white, anonymous and detached. However, Doe does also raise the question of whether serial killing is representative of anything broader at all.

At the beginning of *Copycat* (1995), Helen Hudson (Sigourney Weaver), a world authority on serial killers, gets all the men at a lecture she is giving to stand up; then, if they are not white and are under twenty or over thirty-five, they are to sit down; the remainder, young white adult males, are, she informs her audience, the pool from which 'nine out of ten' serial killers are drawn. Some dispute this widespread statistic, though those who do only manage to demonstrate small increases in the percentages of women and non-white serial killers. Certainly as a cultural categorisation, made by police, psychiatry and popular culture alike, serial killing remains an ostensibly white male phenomenon. To this Doe is no exception.

Serial killers are not only men, they prey specifically on women or socially inferior men (young, black, gay). The serial killer's maleness is misogyny and male supremacism writ large. Yet Doe kills middle-aged white people, four male, three female,[18] rather even-handed, one might say, and without expression of sexual hatred or even apparent interest. It is the case that the selection of victims in relation to sins is resonant of gender in the case of Lust and Pride, and in very old-fashioned ways. Lust is a prostitute, hardly herself guilty of lust itself but rather a vehicle for – or, as some killers of women might put it, an incitement to – male lust. Doe refers to her as 'the disease spreading whore', clearly expressing a traditional disgust with female sexuality. The suffering dwelt on by the film is not the woman's, but the hapless client's screaming, shivering, sweating horror. Similarly, Doe identifies Pride in 'a woman so ugly on the inside that she couldn't bear to go on living if she couldn't be beautiful on the outside' and props her picture at the end of her bed, an emblem of her absorption in her own image. Pride is thus cast in the tired old mould of the association of women with narcissism and vanity. Doe – and quite probably the film itself – is in these ways conventionally, unthinkingly misogynist, but the other murders indicate that he is not driven by hatred of women.

There is a slight implication that as a man Doe is sexually inadequate or possibly homosexual. In the final moments of the film, he tells Mills of going to see Tracy:

I tried to play husband, I tried to taste the life of a simple man. It didn't work out. So I took a souvenir, her pretty head. Because I envy your normal life, it seems that envy is my sin.

Kevin Spacey's performance, the rather prissy lips and precise delivery, the shot of him delicately dunking a tea bag in a cup after his arrest, might add up to a sense of Doe's effeminacy. Failing to have sex with Tracy and envying Mills's normality could thus be taken as indicating impotence or homosexuality. None of this is clear-cut, however, least of all the speech to Mills, which is not only intended to goad him into becoming Wrath (and may therefore be untrue, except in relation to the fact of having killed Tracy) but is said in a tone so ironic as to render that 'seems' utterly ambiguous. As elsewhere, it is just as likely that Doe is happy to mobilise commonplaces about serial killers' virility as that he really envies Mills's normality.

The film seems to make even less of Doe's whiteness than his masculinity, and the issue might not arise at all were it not for the casting of Morgan Freeman as Somerset. Nothing is said about his colour either, nor was he cast because of it. However, the significance of Somerset being black is also reinforced by a number of other, in intention race neutral decisions. The District Attorney, Talbot, is played by Richard Roundtree, iconic star of a cop film series that was making a point about blackness, *Shaft* (1971), and the soundtrack includes, at the Mills's, the title song from another blaxsploitation movie, *Trouble Man* (1972). The use of a silver print (see Chapter 6, 'Sight') tends, Royal Brown suggests,[19] to 'highlight the flesh tones' of black actors, giving them a

greater presence than usual. In this context, the Somerset–Mills duo becomes even more resonant (or counter-resonant) of *Lethal Weapon* et al. Somerset also belongs with two other gifted black investigators, Sidney Poitier in *In the Heat of the Night* (1967) and Freeman himself in *Kiss the Girls* (1997), films which explicitly pit the education, intelligence and good sense of the black investigator against whites who are both stupid and racist. All this may inadvertently flush out something more often shoved under the carpet, that serial killing a white thing.

This is also carried in the association of Doe in the credits sequence with the band Nine Inch Nails, who in turn are associated with multiple murderer Charles Manson (see Chapter 5, 'Sound'), whose messianic vision was founded in part on a belief that black people were hell bent on exterminating whites, thus giving a racial flavour to his mayhem. And then there is Brad Pitt's whiteness. As José Arroyo points out,[20] Pitt 'is a Mid-Western rural white boy, in other words what in American culture passes for average or normal' and his films 'generally stress that he is a White Anglo-Saxon Protestant' by contrasting him to Native American or black people. He also played a white trash serial killer in *Kalifornia* in 1993. I have discussed above the affinity between Doe and Mills. One might say that Pitt-as-Mills unites – and shows the unity of – Pitt's WASP and serial killer roles. If Freeman/Somerset's blackness alerts us to the whiteness of serial killing, Pitt/Mills'ss whiteness perhaps suggests the serial killingness of whiteness.

I'll return to the significance of Doe's masculinity and, especially, his whiteness through a consideration of the qualities of anonymity and detachment. His serial killing is facilitated or even fostered, as most theories of the phenomenon emphasise, by the anonymity of modern, urban life. This is a world in which no-one knows who anyone else is, nor cares, a point underlined by Somerset, telling Mills that women in self-defence classes are taught to yell 'Fire!', not 'Help!' or 'Rape!', since only self-preservation will rouse anyone to come to their rescue. Serial killers are invisible: they look like anyone else and since, in contemporary society, we don't know who anyone else is, they could be anyone else. Doe lives on a drab, characterless corridor in a drab, characterless apartment block. He is unremarkable to look at, not cute like Michael Rooker in *Henry Portrait of a Serial Killer* (1986) or hunky like Pitt in *Kalifornia*, nor pop-eyed like Peter Lorre in *M* (1931) or grotesque like Joe Spinell in *Maniac* (1981). Moreover, until he gives himself up, he is faceless. When Somerset and Mills see him at the end of the corridor outside his door, he is a silhouette of pork-pie hat and three-quarter length mac; throughout the subsequent chase, he is positioned and lit to be nothing but an outlined shape; at the climax, with Mills defenceless on the ground, he appears first as a silhouette reflection in a pool of water

Left: *Shaft*. Right: *Kalifornia*

M

Maniac

*Henry Portrait of a
Serial Killer*

and then twice as an out-of-focus head and hat at the end of an in-focus gun pointing at Mills's off-screen head.

Such literal anonymity is reinforced by his name. John Doe is the name in law for a plaintiff in an action when that person cannot be named, but it has become generalised to mean the American Everyman, as in the film *Meet John Doe* (1941), in which Gary Cooper plays a man called John Doe who is used opportunistically by a newspaper to embody the plight of the ordinary American. In *Seven*, it is not clear whether Doe is a given or chosen name and the ambiguity is reinforced by the fact that he is officially Jonathan not John, but either way it gestures towards the same notion of the anonymous anyone.

Except that it is a male name and, asked to summon up an image of John Doe, it is doubtful that anyone would, except purposefully, come

up with anything other than a white man. White masculinity occupies the space of ordinariness and, in this sense, invisibility. As, following David Lloyd, I have argued elsewhere,[21] the ideal (and never fully realisable) position of power in everyday life in contemporary society is that of notional invisibility, seeing but unseen, unmarked by particularities of class, race or gender, a position that is most nearly and readily occupied by white men.

The ideal personality type that occupies this position is at once characterless – silhouetted, nameless – and emotionally detached and uninvolved. Doe's manner of speech, as delivered by Spacey, conveys both of these aspects. It is grammatically correct, with no use of expletives or colourful vocabulary, and spoken in an even tone, while also at the same time infused with the aural sign of detachment, namely, icy irony. The latter can be terrible, as when he sees the expression on Mills's face on learning that Tracy was pregnant, cocks his head, smiles and says to Somerset with chilling mock sympathy, 'He didn't know.' Doe's colourless delivery permits him to occupy the position of amused disdain.

Detachment means also a lack of felt human connection with others. Such detachment permits Doe's methodical approach and long-term planning. It gives him the lofty indifference that allows him to organise his carnage expressively, arranging the space of the murder scenes (piles of neatly arranged spaghetti sauce tins at Gluttony's, Greed's head laying on law books, hundreds of room deodorants in the form of Christmas trees hanging from the ceiling over Sloth's putrefying body), suggesting a kind of performance art (someone at the discovery of

Sloth says he's like 'some kind of friggin' wax sculpture or something'; the owner of Wild Bill's Leather says he thought Doe 'was one of those performance artists ... the sort of guy that pisses in a cap on stage, then drinks it – performance art'). The chain of murders itself is a work that must, he says in the final car journey, be seen as a whole to be appreciated, 'his masterpiece' as Somerset observes.

All of this, and with it the ability to manipulate and outmanoeuvre the police at every stage, makes him comparable to Hannibal Lecter in Thomas Harris's two books (*Red Dragon* 1981, *The Silence of the Lambs* 1988) and the two films based on them (*Manhunter* 1986, *The Silence of the Lambs* 1991). There are marked class differences between them: Lecter is a successful professional who appreciates fine things, food, perfume, music (and, in the film versions, is played by British actors, a group long used in Hollywood to convey posh nastiness); Doe is an unemployed man whose apartment reveals an autodidact, an obsessive writer and reader lacking the cultural background to weld it all into a witty *Weltanschauung*. Both however are amused, superior, cold geniuses of death, the apotheosis of what has been historically a white masculine ideal.

I have forced this reading, in a manner often necessary to see the specificity of whiteness concealed in its apparently non-specific ordinariness. Doe's whiteness is not raised explicitly by the film itself, though it is brought out by decisions of casting and stock selection that had quite other purposes. The implication, which I have explored elsewhere,[22] is that there is something about white masculinity in the anomic conditions of contemporary societies that leads to serial killing. However, *Seven* does not directly address this, and moreover also deploys terms common in serial killer discourse that cast doubt on the idea that serial killers are socially meaningful at all.

This is at issue in the debate about whether the serial killer is a product of society, or whether he isn't, on the contrary, outside of it, radically other.[23] The commonest form of the latter, articulated at several points by Mills, is the notion of insanity. The script has Mills slip between the different valencies of this position in a way that is entirely typical, mixing potentially sympathetic terms like 'mentally ill', 'insane' or 'a lunatic' with, in the same sentence or exchange, abusive ones like 'fuckin' crazy', 'a nutbag', 'the fuckin' freak'. Speaking to Doe in the car journey he starts off blandly but soon escalates into a savage riff:

When a person is insane, as you clearly are, do you know that you're insane? Maybe you're just sittin' around, reading *Guns and Ammo*, masturbating in your own faeces, do you just stop and go, 'Wow! It's just amazing how fuckin' crazy I really am!', yeah? You guys do that?

Doe replies, with characteristic deadly accuracy, 'It's more comfortable for you to label me insane.' To consider serial killing beyond the pale of normal sanity is to distance oneself from the implication that it might express impulses in all of us (or all of some of us, white men). As Somerset says to Mills, it's 'dismissive to call him a lunatic, don't make that mistake'.

Somerset and Doe are however making slightly different points. Both are saying that serial killing is not the madness of the other, but Doe suggests that he is doing it because he was 'chosen' (by God), whereas Somerset is arguing that Doe is 'just a man', that in talking about serial killing, 'we're talking about everyday life'. The debate between Somerset and Mills – about whether Doe as serial killer is socially representative – crops up on and off throughout *Seven*. It is not resolved by the film at the level of the unresolvable oppositions of sanity: madness, normal: abnormal. It remains an ever open issue. Yet we may make some sense of Doe's representativeness by considering a paradoxical way of conceptualising the relation between serial killers and society, namely, that far from being against or outside society, as embodied in the law, they in fact over-identify with it.

The commonest form of this, from Thomas Neill Cream[24] and perhaps 'Jack the Ripper' to Peter Sutcliffe, the Yorkshire Ripper, is the murder of prostitutes, killing the morally despised or, as many feminists argued at the time of the Sutcliffe murders, simply killing the last word in female despicability,[25] enacting the view of women under patriarchy. In Andrea Dworkin's words:

In male culture, police are heroic and so are outlaws; males who enforce standards are heroic and so are those who violate them. The conflicts between these groups embody the male commitment to violence … [but it] is a mistake to view the warring factions of male culture as genuinely distinct from one another: in fact, [they] operate in near-perfect harmony to keep women at their mercy.[26]

With a serial killer like Sutcliffe, the warring factions are indeed embodied in one man and his 'crusade' against women. The idea, not necessarily in a femicidal context, is played on in serial killer texts where the authority on, and thus leader in the fight against, the serial killer turns out to be the killer himself (e.g. *The Unsuspected* 1947), sometimes a policeman (*The Eyes of Laura Mars* 1978, *Kiss the Girls* 1997, *Nightwatch* 1998) or a psychiatrist, as in Robert Bloch's legendary short story, 'Yours Truly, Jack the Ripper',[27] the cult Peter Walker film *House of Whipcord* (1974), *Dressed to Kill* (1980) and Hannibal Lecter.

Doe does not kill against womankind, nor is he in a position of authority, yet he may none the less be identified with the law. In a discussion of the film at a conference in Naples, Lidia Curti referred several times to 'the preacher'. At first, I could not understand whom she meant, until I realised it was Doe. She had picked up Somerset's cue: the murders, he says, are Doe's sermons to us. In Victor's flat, a cop leans over what he believes is a dead body and whispers, 'You got what you deserved.' Cops are supposed to administer what is deserved, but Doe has taken upon himself to do the work that they fail to do. He identifies with the moral code of society, a Christian society that is failing to be Christian – it is Doe who upholds the law (as he sees it) to which the society is supposed to be committed.

Doe as serial killer represents the ideals of society, both in being typical of its highest point of aspiration, cold white masculinity, and in enacting the values that Christian Western society claims to believe in. But he is also representative of something more metaphysical. For another resolution of the like us/not like us debate about serial killers is that we are all in sin. Doe knows this. He avenges particular sins in the persons of individuals in order to make an example of them, but he also knows – at any rate he is too clever not to see this logic – that if everyone is a sinner, then so is he. So he engineers his own death. This act declares that the serial killer is indeed representative, because he is, like everyone else, a sinner.

5 Sound

I saw *Seven* recently at a cinema in the West End of London, and I was extremely disappointed to discover that this outstanding film was accompanied by sound of appalling quality. [...] I realise that the mood of the film is particularly dark, moody and that clarity of image and sound was not the director's main aim. However, the extent to which the sound was obscured goes beyond the concept of artistic licence.

(Letter in *Screen International*[28] from Hugo Ruiz)

'Would you please be quiet?'

(Somerset to Mills at the Gluttony murder scene)

You hear *Seven* before you see it. Briefly over darkness there is the sound of traffic, of horns sounding at different registers, and of television talk programmes, probably news, the sound quality recognisable even while you cannot quite make out what is being said. Then the image fades up on Somerset in his kitchen. Similarly, the film ends with a fade to black with the sound of helicopter blades continuing over.

Such sound montage runs throughout the film, a soft cacophony of cars (motors, horns, brakes), voices (people in the next apartment or on the street, television, domestic and police radio, walkie talkies), footsteps down the hall, snatches of music (radio, records, musak), dogs, water pipes (knocks, hiss), squeaks (kids, rats, floorboards), bottles falling over, planes, helicopters, subway trains and all the other aural detritus of city life, and rain. This is all elaborately crafted, albeit based upon actually occurring sounds. It is not really naturalism. On the one hand, just pointing a microphone out of the window would not produce such an effect. On the other, we do not in life choose to hear all this sound around us, we do not attend to the patina of noise around us, and most films minimise it down to a vague 'ambient sound'. In *Seven*, it is not minimised, it is insistently and remorselessly present.

There is no decipherable speech during the first forty seconds of the film, showing Somerset getting ready to go out, just sounds. Inside, any sound Somerset makes is clearly related to what we see him doing (putting a mug in the sink, pouring leftover coffee down the drain, walking across the kitchen, pulling his tie up to his neck) and is also very quiet: the sounds he makes are deliberate and minimal. Outside the apartment, the dominant sound over the cars and voices is a siren. Given that *Seven* is a thriller, we are most likely to assign the siren to a police car and it might even be the one going to the scene of the crime to which the film cuts almost immediately. However, as with Somerset's quiet precision, the siren also relates to the wider sense of sound in the film.

Just before the opening credits, after he and Mills have met at a domestic murder scene, Somerset lies in bed. There is as ever the muffled racket of the city, notably of voices raised in conflict. Somerset puts out his hand and sets a metronome going, and the clamour outside becomes louder and more echoey as he none the less falls asleep. The metronome is an oasis of controlled, orderly sound that enables him to sleep. Later, when the police captain brings Somerset news of the second murder, he (Somerset) stops typing on the word 'Greed', a cessation of deliberate noise (emphasised by an overhead shot of his hands freezing at the keyboard) that underscores his pricking his ears up. He then asks a man scraping his name off the door to stop doing so, putting an end to a tiny but needlessly intrusive noise. He cannot halt the sounds of the city and the rain, but he can take responsibility for the sounds he is able to control.

Throughout the film, Somerset's speech is also spare, quiet, to the point. This is in part a function of Morgan Freeman's expressively minimalist acting style – much of Somerset's script was cut because of it,[29] just as Mills's was elaborated for Brad Pitt. The difference in acting style also articulates the symbolically significant difference between the characters. Where Somerset speaks when he needs to or remains silent, and only makes quiet, purposeful or unavoidable sounds, Mills is constant hubbub. There is a scene of him getting up immediately after the credits; after he's put on a tie, he stubs his foot against a metal object on the floor, exactly the unnecessary, careless noise absent from the scene with Somerset minutes before. At the Gluttony scene, he chatters, talks about another case, jokes, says 'Woops!' when he sees the victim's feet tied together, until Somerset asks him to be quiet and eventually to leave. Subsequently in the car, he keeps clicking at a ball-point pen. And so on throughout the film. If Somerset seeks to keep the noise of the world at bay and to add only what is strictly necessary to it, Mills adds to it unthinkingly all the time.

Mills's early morning scene, like Somerset's, fades up on the sound of a police siren. Throughout the film, sound reminds us that crime and violence are ever present: police cars, television reports, squabbling and screams, children watching a cavorting cartoon in the apartment through which Mills chases Doe. It is the habitual background of life. At the pre-credits murder scene, the duty cop reports, 'The neighbours heard them screaming at each other like for two hours, there was nothing new, then they heard the gun go off, both barrels.' The sound of aggression, conflict, hysteria, is something we have learnt to become indifferent to, because, as Doe says of sin, 'it's common, it's trivial, [and so] we tolerate it morning, noon and night,' or at any rate until it's too late.

When Somerset sets his metronome going, the camera tracks slowly in on to close-up. There is a crash of thunder, which eclipses the sound of the metronome and then segues into a synthesised crash and the beginnings of the rhythms of the credits sequence soundtrack. This can be described in musical terms: a repeated, rather throbbing bass figure, later overlaid with a faster, blurred, more metallic beat in a higher register; the piece organised as a fugue brought to a close with a single, sung phrase and a loud, very reverberative single deep drum beat; the whole recorded with a strong echo quality. However, the sounds themselves combine those recognisably produced by what are conventionally deemed musical instruments – drum, cymbal, bass, synthesiser, voice – with others that would not be – the squeak of plastic, scratching with chalk, a match's flair, doors opening on creaky hinges and sounds familiar from space movies ('weird' electronic descending notes, · the burps and beeps of interplanetary radio). In other words, music and 'noise' are fused, indistinguishable one from the other. The remorseless hubbub of the city bleeds into the music of the credits.

This is entirely appropriate. First, the music accompanies close-up shots of John Doe about his work, not killing but preparing and recording – the credit sequence takes us into the mind of the killer. This is the special appropriateness of the sung phrase, 'You get me closer to God', cried out of the tumult of sound, salvation plucked from sin. Secondly, the track is performed by Nine Inch Nails, making reference to the track 'Closer' on the album *The Downward Spiral* (1994). In fact it bears little specific relation to the track, beyond taking the sung phrase from it; the significance is much more the recognisable sound of a group notoriously fascinated with Charles Manson and the controversial fact that the album was recorded in his house. Thus this soundtrack blurs the distinction between music and noise, and relates both to sin.

The closing credits sequence, David Bowie's 'The Hearts [*sic*] Filthy Lesson', works to some extent in a similar way, aurally and allusively. Though instrumentally more conventional, there is an overlay of industrial sounds. It is taken from the album *1. Outside* (1995), subtitle *The Nathan Adler Diaries: a hyper cycle*. The album booklet presents parts of said diary, written by a detective specialising in 'art-murder', real killings (as of the horrifically described 'art-ritual murder of Baby Grace Blue. … It was definitely murder – but was it art?') and 'concept-muggings', all placed historically in relation to such figures as 'the Viennese castrationists', Guy Bourdin and Damien Hirst, to which we might add Helmut Newton and *The Eyes of Laura Mars*, Brett Easton Ellis's *American Psycho* and, as discussed in Chapter 4, 'Seriality', Doe himself as performance artist. 'The Hearts Filthy Lesson' is signalled on the album 'To be sung by Detective Nathan Adler'; *Alfred* Adler was a psycho-analytic theorist most popularly understood to deal with the violence of the human psyche; the images accompanying the track in *Seven* resemble Doe's obsessive collages but also the chalk writing on the board in the police headquarters – in other words, authority and the law are folded into the song's bleak vision alongside cruelty and vice.

'Closer' and 'The Hearts Filthy Lesson' take us into the heart of darkness, and this is also true of the music score by Howard Shore (whose previous credits include killer movies such as *The Silence of the*

Lambs, Single White Female 1992 and *Sliver* 1993). It is characterised by: a use of what are widely perceived as dark musical elements (low registers; brass, basses, cellos), sometimes set off by very high, 'sinister' string notes; for much of the time de-emphasised rhythm, the music insinuating and spreading its darkness; strongly marked rhythms for action sequences (the descent on Victor's apartment, Mills's pursuit of Doe) and the climax; and tonal progression that endlessly promises melody and completion but never really delivers it, drawing one endlessly onwards through the darkness. In its first introduction, outside the Gluttony murder scene, it emerges imperceptibly within the sound of heavy rain and a truck passing – if, unlike Nine Inch Nails, it is more traditionally 'musical', its introduction none the less connects it to the city's sodden clamour. Once inside the house, the music eclipses outside sound, with only the sounds of human movement (footfalls, clothes rustling) and speech heard against it. The deeper the detectives enter into the house, the more menacing and dominant the music seems to become.

Throughout the film, the introduction of the score is triggered by the encounter with Doe and his work: Mills standing over Greed written in blood on the floor; Somerset turning to look at the plastic strips found in the Fat Boy's stomach that the chief leaves for him and paying a return visit to the victim's apartment; Mills and Somerset returning to Gould's apartment to look at a wrongly hung painting;[30] moving in on Victor's corpse; the investigation of Doe's and Pride's apartments; the ride to the last two bodies. Only the music for the entry to the sex club, site of the Lust murder, is not Shore's sombre brass and strings; this is heavy rock, reminiscent of Nine Inch Nails, but in fact by the film's sound designer Ren Klyce and Steve Boedekker. Hence it retains the associations of 'Closer', while also being unsurprisingly close to the film's relentless aural montage.

The score may be monotonal, but it is not monotonous. The repeated introduction of this restricted musical palette in relation to Doe's work establishes it as redolent of sin. Variations enable it to express aspects of sin such as energy, insinuation and intensity. The first is apparent in the action sequences.

For the descent on Victor's apartment the variations on Shore's dark colours include: driving and melodic spiralling for the cops leaving the briefing and the cars speeding out of the precinct garage; urgent, staccato chords for the arrival at the apartment block and the cops dressed like militia storming the stairs; mysterious and tense held chords for moving along the corridor to the apartment door, climaxing musically on a track in on the door; a crash for breaking and entering. The music is overlaid with the louder sounds of the police chief's echoing briefing, doors opening and slamming, feet clattering, cars hitting the ground and tyres screeching in the rush. Despite the differences in tempo, much the same music is being used for cops as is elsewhere used for the killer, with here the music subordinated to the noise. This is appropriate. The glee with which Victor is pursued is comparable with Doe's mania. As Somerset remarks of the cops, 'They love this.'

In another action sequence, when Mills chases Doe, the music provides a remorseless underlying pounding, sometimes eclipsed by the sound of shooting, rain and human movement. At two moments, when Mills first bursts outside onto a fire escape into the deluge and when he is felled to the ground and crawls through the water and rainfall, an unexpected falling phrase in the higher strings gives the sequence an astonishing sense of agony in the Christian sense, suffering of cosmic significance.

The insinuation of sin is suggested musically throughout the film, where the music is not 'mickey-moused' in a one-to-one way to character, camera movement or editing, but rather seeps in, sometimes hidden in the ambient sound, spreading itself out alongside the image. There is a more symbolic effect of insinuation in the score when Mills cuddles up to Tracy in bed, the last time we see her in the film. The music is tender and intimate, yet with enough of the brooding, menacing qualities to hint at Tracy's destiny without drawing attention to it (cf. Chapter 3, 'Structure'). Even when Mills is being most caring, in contact with an embodiment of goodness in the film, sin will not let the soundtrack alone.

Intensity is expressed in the final sequence, with the recognition of sin in Mills. This is one of the few sections of the film where the music is

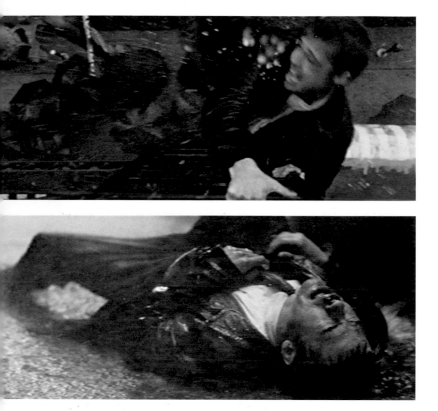

Mills's agony

to a certain extent 'mickey-moused' (though the cheeriness of the term hardly does justice to the grimness of the effect). Throughout the final twenty minutes or so of the film, the music seems to be ever rising, the melodic line going higher, the harmonic progression approaching climactic resolution, getting louder. Yet it never really gets higher, does not resolve nor even really get much louder. As Christa Lykke Christensen at the University of Copenhagen said to me, the music seems like it's about to burst but never does. Then, when the van driver delivers the box, there is a very long, slow fade on a sustained note. There is no music as Somerset looks, opens, investigates the box. The music comes back with a deep, staccato, jabbing chord on an alarmingly swift pan to Somerset turning sharply to look at Mills and Doe in the distance; each subsequent cut (between Somerset, Mills with Doe, and the box) is accompanied by this chord, with an overlay of high, sinister sounds. This pattern, subtly varied and with interspersed passages of the slower, dark, spreading music of the rest of the film, continues for the remainder of the sequence, eventually getting louder, ending on long sustained, mounting notes as Mills shoots Doe, as he is drawn inexorably – or what the music makes feel is inexorably – into his sin. The music only ends with the slamming of the police car door on the psychologically and morally destroyed Mills.

There are in the diegetic music exceptions to the association of music with sin. Tracy and Somerset are characters who bond together and are not implicated in white male seriality; both play classic African-American music – Tracy has 'Trouble Man' by Marvin Gaye and 'Straight No Chaser' by Thelonius Monk on at the dinner party, Somerset is listening to 'Now's the Time' by Charlie Parker on the radio when she phones him. In the library scene, where Somerset investigates the literature on the deadly sins, the cops put on Bach's 'Air on a G String'. Though emanating from a portable radio, the sound quality has the clarity and amplitude of the film's own score. The film cuts between Somerset and Mills, pursuing their rather different sets of evidence, Somerset literature and theology, Mills photos of the crimes; yet the Bach carries over both. Only occasionally are ambient sounds heard over it – the cops laughing, Somerset's light footfalls, the television when Mills gives up for the night. The calm and rationality of Bach embrace them both, an oasis of literally and metaphorically uncontaminated sound that only draws attention to the unremitting sense of aural defilement in the rest of the film.

6 Sight

Sometimes the producer came to me and said, 'You know, it's a bit dark.' I say, 'Yes, I know.'
(Darius Khondji on shooting *Seven*)[31]

Long is the way and hard
That out of hell leads up to light.
(Milton, *Paradise Lost*; quotation left by Doe at Gluttony murder scene)

Some people, when they learnt that I was writing about *Seven*, said that they had not been able to bring themselves to see it, to which I replied that they need not have worried since you don't see anything. Written down the exchange sounds barmy, but we all knew what we meant. They had heard that the film was full of gruesome things and I was assuring them that one did not actually see any of them, no acts of killing, no writhing and bleeding corpses, neither splatter nor gore. I might however have meant it differently and more negatively, for one complaint sometimes levelled against *Seven* is that it is so dark that you literally can't see anything. I want to look at both these aspects of seeing in this section.

It is not the case that you see nothing horrid whatsoever in *Seven*. We do see the corpses of the Gluttony and Sloth murders. Though the screen time cannot be much more than a minute in total, they stick in the mind. Many reviewers dwelt on the memorable spectacle of the Fat Boy's huge body on the mortuary slab, sluiced down with water so that the white flesh with stretched purple veining looks like marble, and of Victor, almost literally nothing but skin and bones, with yellowing, protuberant teeth, dilated eyes and beetles crawling over him. The shock of the sight of these then does for the other bodies that are seen only in long shot, black and white police photos or not at all. Shock is also carried in the density with which all the bodies are represented: each was played by a real person, special make-up effects (by Rob Bottin) were lavished on their bodies, their living spaces and Doe's arrangement of it were meticulously recreated and we are told just enough about the manner of death to be able to visualise it. Thus although in fact we see practically nothing of gore, its presence is forcefully conveyed.

To this extent, *Seven* is in line with much contemporary horror cinema. Traditionally, horror resided in what the monster, whatever it was, looked like or the fear it induced in the characters; now it is as often in its effect on the body, the horror of the damaged, distressed, suffering body. The turn to such body horror in recent cinema has been related by several commentators[32] to two aspects of contemporary culture. First, there is a perception that the body is in our times ever less safe from injury and mutilation; in particular, we live in a world whose anonymity and indifference have spawned and facilitated the serial killer. Like others,[33] Doe in *Seven* seems invisible and potentially anywhere, he enters domestic spaces with ease, passes unnoticed through the city – a pervasive invisibility to which only these terrible cadavers are witness. Secondly, there is the part-Puritan, part profit-driven obsession with the body, and with that a heightened dread of disease, death and decay. Is it chance that the two hideous bodies actually shown in *Seven* are those that tap into the most obvious manifestations of this, over-eating (Gluttony) and under-exercising (Sloth), twin horrors of US body fascism?

However, despite the minute of unforgettable gore, *Seven* does not dwell on body horror. In part this works to make things even more terrible. As horror film criticism has often insisted, it may be more frightening not to see things, to allow the imagination free rein and to rely on it always to outstrip what can actually be shown. Certainly the unseen deaths of the hooker and Tracy horrify me more than the graphically seen Fat Boy and Victor.

Not dwelling on the corpses also draws attention to the grand design of the killer and the film itself, to a kind of metaphysical abstraction giving meaning to these bleeding pieces of earth. At times, even what we do see seems to evoke this. The first shot of the Gluttony corpse in the autopsy room is taken from above at a roughly 45 degree

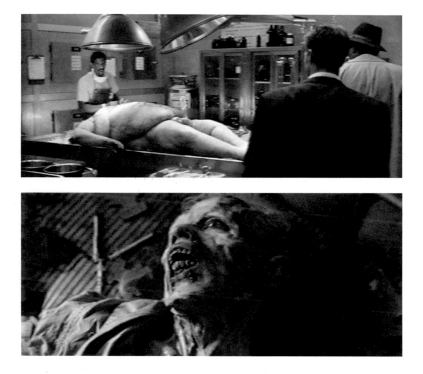

angle to the corpse; it shows just part of the torso, with this expanse of
nacreous white, marbled with pink and purple and splotched with red,
only identifiable as a body by a side of the chest visible across the top left
corner and the chin and right armpit protruding into the frame. The
framing seems more intent on rendering an abstraction of torment than
insisting on it as a wretched body.

Such abstraction may be a relief from the disgusting, squalid
nature of the killings, in effect buying into Doe's grandiosity. It may allow
us, as virtually all serial killing texts do, fact or fiction, whatever the
medium, to avoid the reality of the victims' experience.[34] Only the
doctor's words on Victor ('he's experienced about as much pain and
suffering of anyone I've encountered, give or take') begin to open up the
perspective of the victim, and even these are transmuted into ironic

Top: 'the fat boy' (Gluttony). Bottom: Victor (Sloth)

metaphysics ('and he still has hell to look forward to'). As discussed in Chapter 7, 'Salvation', this abstraction may be what appeals to many audiences, giving the film a philosophical air at odds with the empiricism of, say, *M*, *10 Rillington Place*, *Maniac* or *Henry Portrait of a Serial Killer*. It also robs us of some of the pleasures of splatter and gore, bodies torn open, bleeding, innards spilling out, limbs twisted or severed, what Isabel Cristina Pinedo calls 'the spectacle of the wet death'.[35] Pinedo suggests that the point of such seeing-it-all body horror movies resides in both mastering and/or (safely) surrendering to the horrific sights, either daring yourself to look, to go on looking, toughing it out, or screaming, letting go, grossing out. *Seven*'s reticence denies us this, which means that, for all its metaphysics, it also gives us no respite from the terror of the fragility of the body, no visceral defence against the materiality of torment.

If it is not entirely true that you don't see, leave alone sense, anything nasty in *Seven*, it is also not true that it is unremittingly dark. While it both opens and closes (before the final credits) on a black screen, it does in its unfolding get progressively lighter. However, the more literally light it gets, the more symbolically dark it becomes.

Two of the key personnel on *Seven* have a track record on the caliginous. David Fincher's previous work included not only *Alien*³ (1992), the grimmest, dankest, gloomiest of the series, but also music videos like 'Janie's Got a Gun' for Aerosmith (dramatically dark, lots of silhouetting, large areas of shadow surrounding vivid but deep blue and red light, torch light that does not really give light (very *Seven*)) and three for Madonna, each referencing renowned instances of photographic chiaroscuro: 'Express Yourself' (1989, Madonna in ultra-white, gleaming apartment contrasting to *Metropolis*-like underworld of hunky men wet from industrial rain), 'Oh Father' (1990, brooding, *Citizen Kane* derived imagery) and 'Vogue' (1991, high contrast black-and-white fashion plate and Hollywood glamour imagery). Cinematographer Darius Khondji's feeling for contrast and darkness is evident in *Trésor des îles chiennes* (1990, a black-and-white film printed on Kodak soundtrack stock, which creates heightened chiaroscuro with blacks 'like China ink'),[36] *Delicatessen* (1991, the first film in which he used the resilvering process discussed below) and *La Cité des enfants perdus* (1995, trying out another high-contrast technique).

Khondji seems to have determined the base means of *Seven*'s 'crepuscular aesthetic'[37] with certain fundamental cinematographic decisions: Panavision Primo lenses ('very sharp, very graphic and contrasty') and Kodak stocks 93 for interiors ('all the gritty stuff'), 45 for daytime and 87 for night-time exteriors (giving especially 'rich' blacks).[38] The processing used a resilvering technique. Silver is normally taken out of prints, partly to save money, partly because a blander, less contrasted look is believed to be what people want. In the technique used for *Seven*, the silver is put back in the processing – the stock 'run first through colour baths then re-souped as black-and-white',[39] making rich, black blacks and desaturated colours. Unfortunately most prints of the film do not use the process, making a cult of screenings of 'the silver print'.

Within this dark register, and with Fincher and Khondji collaborating very closely with designer Arthur Max, the colour signature of *Seven* is oligochromatic, that is, composed of a very limited, closely related range of colours: white, cream, grey, slate, ochre, beige, brown, black and dirty, acidic greens. The latter are often used for visible light sources, lampshades and light coming through windows; the detectives' torches give off blue-grey light. When a colour outside the range occurs, it sets off the uniformity of tone. This is sometimes a purely formal effect: red, green and blue lights, distorted by the rain, are glimpsed through the windows as Mills and Somerset drive from the Gluttony murder scene, reinforcing the remorselessness of the overall colouring. Somerset, and later Mills, uses forensic gloves of a pretty, bright green colour, not dissimilar to the office glass lampshades seen at other points, and notably in the library sequence, where the rows of blue-green shades give off a pinkish light. Such attractive, synthetic pastels not only simultaneously relieve and draw attention to the oligochromaticism, they are also associated with the character, Somerset, who most conscientiously seeks enlightenment in the encroaching gloom.

The darkness of exteriors is heightened by two features: the masked sun and the rain, so that one would be hard put to it to identify

this as Los Angeles. There are somewhat varying accounts concerning the implacable rain. In one interview,[40] Fincher says it was 'really a purely pragmatic decision': they only had a limited time for shooting with Brad Pitt and couldn't risk there being some continuity-challenging rain in some shots. As it was raining some of time, they had to make it look like rain all of the time. In another interview,[41] it seems a more conscious artistic choice:

> I liked the idea of the rain. I was looking for something so that there wasn't any escape. You couldn't go, 'I'm in this horrible, cramped, dark room and I'm going to go outside' because outside isn't that much better.

Pitt himself speaks of the continual rain machines.[42] Whatever else, it was not like this because it just happened to be raining. The rain casts a pall over everything, but it also has other resonances. Like sin, rain soaks, it gets in everywhere, there's nowhere to go. This is the rain of film noir and dystopian science fiction, of *Blade Runner* (1982) and the future sequences of *The Terminator* films (1984, 1991). This is rain as pollution, the rain that humankind has produced.

The murder scenes draw out and emphasise different colours from the basic palette. Gluttony is the darkest, with brownish lampshades casting small pools of light on sallowing wallpaper and torches stabbing light into the darkness without illuminating very much (such that Mills comments jokingly to the doctor, 'In this room light's a problem'); Khondji suggests the effect is that of light on grease in a pitch black space. Greed features a room of brown wood and cream walls, lit by muted internal lights and, the first time it is seen, dull daylight from outside broken into soft shadows (notably in the last, overhead shot of the scene, Mills standing over the word Greed on the floor). Sloth is tinged with green, 'a very necrotic, green scene', according to Khondji, 'like being under the bottom of a river … a moist, fungal look'. Lust is bathed in infernal red neon, at times looking like a negative in a darkroom. Pride, on the other hand, is all white walls, sheets and tiling, everything spotted with blood, and light coming from outside without casting any shadows (again most evident in the final tableau of Somerset and Mills standing over the body with the word 'Pride' between them). Khondji sees these variations in relation to Doe's stage management of the scenes, which suggests the serial killer as performance artist idea.[43]

The dark in Western culture is oppressive, dangerous and a sign of wickedness. The rigour and remorselessness of *Seven*'s darkness serve

not only to make it frightening and sinister, but are also redolent of the film's vision of the encroachment and profundity of sin. Seen in ideal conditions (a silver print in a properly darkened auditorium), it should be impossible to discern the contours of the screen, the film's darkness reaching out to embrace us.

Yet the film does gradually get lighter. Scenes like the dinner at the Mills's, the Thursday meeting in the police station and, as already noted, the Lust and especially Pride murder sites introduce more light into the film. Immediately after the latter, there is the first exterior shot in sunlight, an almost startling sight emphasised by Mills looking up at the sun as he steps out of the car, at last providing stellar illumination of Brad Pitt's face. The film cuts back to a long, tracking shot of Mills and Somerset walking to the police station door, sunlight glistening off the car windows and road surface. A cab pulls up near the camera and Doe gets out (although we will only know this half a minute later). The irony of the film's increasing light is all there – we get full sunshine when we finally see the killer.

The film remains light thereafter, apart from the very last shots (before the final credits). The last two deaths are enacted in a wide open space (the antithesis of the city), with blue sky and ochre stubble filling much of the frame, and in clear sunlight. However, as Chris Darke puts it, this 'wasteland light … is not that of clarity and redemption but of blinding, disorienting bleakness'.[44] The irony does not just reside in the

use of full light at the nadir of despair. The script specifies that it is seven in the evening; the low light and longish shadows thus suggest twilight and its associations: closure, decline, melancholy. The wasteland setting is beneath high pylons, in scale and outline comparable to the city, but open. Yet the openness creates criss-cross patterns that may recall the grille in the preceding car journey and also prevent the police in their helicopters hearing what is being said (via the wires on Mills and Somerset). The openness is not really open, any more than the light really enlightens.

On Saturday, the sixth night, in a single overhead shot, Mills snuggles up to Tracy in bed, whispering 'I love you so much.' The *mise en scène* is all white: sheets, Tracy's vest, Mills's T-shirt and bandaged arm; white early morning light streaks across them. Yet for all that, it is still a very dark image – the streaking light only more emphasising the deeply shadowed whiteness of most of the image. Darkness gets in everywhere.

7 Salvation

**'The killer had a gun, he put that thing on me, he told me to fuck her
... and I did.** I fucked her, oh God, oh God, oh God, he had a gun in
my mouth, the fucking gun was in my throat, fuck! Oh God, God,
please help me.'
(Lust's client)

'Oh God, oh God, oh.'
(Mills on realising Tracy and their child are dead)

In a preview of the first screening of *Seven* on BBC television, the *Radio
Times* referred to it as 'possibly the gloomiest film ever made' and Barry
Norman, Britain's best-known film critic, commented that its 'bleak
climax is much too hard on viewers, depriving them even of the final
comfort they fully deserve'.[45] There is indeed no comfort anywhere in
Seven, though it's doubtful that its desolate view of humanity would
suggest that we might 'deserve' such a thing.

Where might such comfort come from? The traditional comfort of
a police film is the solution of a crime and the capture of its perpetrator.
This provides not only the psychic satisfaction of completion but a
reassurance that crime can be kept at bay. *Seven* denies us this. It is true
that we know who did it and he is dead; in the most obvious sense, there
is the most rigorous closure, emphasised by it being also the completion
of a pattern. Yet the very excessiveness of the closure of the plot serves
only to draw attention to the never-ending world of sin that has
throughout been its accompaniment and rationale.

Moreover, the closure is not achieved by the police. The greatest
show of policing in the film, the descent on Victor, merely delivers
another victim. Somerset and Mills do track Doe down to his apartment,
but fail to catch him. On the contrary, he gives himself up and then
succeeds in destroying Mills. The endings desired by the studio (Somerset
and Mills rescuing Tracy in the nick of time, or Somerset shooting
Doe) would have delivered the satisfactory sense that crime can be

solved and justice done; but neither of these is the ending of the film we have.

This is because the film is not working primarily on the level of crime but sin. Crime deals with those manifestations of sin that society takes it upon itself to condemn and punish. This sometimes leads us to think of crime and sin as separable. Indeed, this very distinction was much manifested in the wake of the Starr report on President Clinton's affair with Monica Lewinsky – he'd admitted he'd sinned, but had he committed crimes? However, this Protestant and post-Enlightenment distinction is irrelevant to *Seven*, whose ending actually and symbolically incorporates crime (criminal and law enforcer) into sin. This shifts the whole matter of comfort onto the metaphysical plane that the discourse of sin has all along indicated, where comfort becomes a matter of salvation.

Seven makes reference to three forms of salvation: religion, culture and human goodness. However, it only believes in religion's diagnosis rather than its cure, culture merely affirms bleakness, albeit giving it grandeur, and human goodness is shown to be desperately weak in the face of sin.

Religion is a strong presence in the film – in Doe's seven deadly sins conceit, the library sequence and other references discussed below. It might offer two forms of relief: the promise of actual salvation, or,

failing that, a way of making sense of the world's iniquity that gives it transcendent, cosmic significance, that gives it point.

The relief of literal salvation is almost wholly absent. The Bible, notably the Gospels with their emphasis on the possibilities of virtue and redemption, is never referred to. The canonical texts pored over by Somerset are presented only in terms of their concern with sin: St Thomas Aquinas (Somerset: 'He wrote about the seven deadly sins'), the *Divine Comedy*'s Purgatory not Paradise, Milton's *Paradise Lost* not *Regained*, the Parson's tale, a sermon on sin, rather than the more genial, down to earth Christianity of the other *Canterbury Tales* (and without reference to the fact that the Parson elaborates upon how to avoid sin). The only possible reference to salvation is in the large red neon cross and the standing crucifix hanging on the wall in Doe's bedroom. The cross is the sign of redemption par excellence in Christian iconography, but it is also a sign of suffering for human sin, a transcendent condensation of wickedness. In its fleetingly seen fiery redness in the dark of Doe's apartment, and in the absence of any other reference to salvation, the crucifix seems more part of the second form of relief religion may offer: giving sin cosmic significance.

The film treats this perception gravely. The library sequence does not just explain Doe's acts but immerses us in the iconography and discourse of sin and punishment. The seriousness with which Somerset, the touchstone of value in the film, takes the texts, especially compared to Mills's resort to Cliff's *Pass Notes*, in an environment not invaded by the usual aural pollution and accompanied by the archetypal serenity of Bach's 'Air on a G String', suggests that this is an understanding of the world embraced by the film. This is not the same as Christian belief in it however.

Explicit faith is associated with Doe: his deployment of the sins ('his sermons to us', says Somerset), his crucifixes, his use of the phrase, 'The Lord works in mysterious ways' in response to Somerset's asking him if the murders constitute his doing 'God's good work'. Faith is thus associated with the character whose deeds are also the most cruel and terrible in the film. This itself might not signal a lack of belief on the film's part. Doe's excessive identification with the Law of God could be seen as an aspect of his over-identification with Law in general (see Chapter 4, 'Seriality'). It is the actual handling of the representation of Christianity that destabilises it as a point of true understanding.

I have previously suggested (Chapter 1, 'Sin') that the formulation of sin in terms of seven deadly ones is archaic, out of kilter with the wider presentation of sin in the film itself. Similarly, it is not clear what the canonical texts deliver beyond a general sense of wickedness, perhaps no deeper than that available from Cliff's *Notes*. Mills rejects a full engagement with the texts at his mortal peril, but they are not used as a source of imagery or interpretation in the film.

When Doe says, 'The Lord works in mysterious ways,' Kevin Spacey laces it with irony, aware of the phrase as cliché, his eyes looking off to his right, turned away from Somerset's quizzical gaze as if in acknowledgment that Doe can't convince Somerset that he's really doing God's work because he can't convince himself. The neon crucifix seems excessive, in a way that is perhaps one of the few errors of judgement in the film. Its red light stands out in a film so darkly oligochromatic and its size dwarfs the bare iron single bed beneath it, itself suggestive of religious asceticism. It all seems to be a mobilisation of fundamentalist iconography from the repertoire of serial killer imagery on a par with what Doe himself does in relation to Victor/Sloth. The colour, size and cliché of the image, in a sequence supposedly taking us inside Doe's mentality, seem naff, suggesting a faltering at the very moment of presenting the central symbol of Christian belief.

Religion in *Seven* is archaic or fanatical and faith is presented in uncertain and ironic ways. We are left with the feeling of a world at the very nadir of iniquity, without the comfort even of transcendent explanation. Jonathon Bignell relates this to the notion of post-modern apocalypse, an end-of-the-world, things-have-never-been-worse feeling without the explanatory or redemptive frameworks that have hitherto accompanied apocalyptic thought.[46] Perhaps Doe understands this. When Mills finally 'becomes Wrath' and puts his gun to Doe's head, Spacey/Doe closes his eyes and smiles, an expression of the ecstasy of consummation. His apocalypse at least has the perfect, complete meaning he has created for it.

Perhaps this is the significance of the other important religious reference in the film, the phrase 'You get me closer to God!' over the end of the opening credits sequence. It is associated, visually and aurally, with Doe. But what God can this be from a band like Nine Inch Nails? In the version of 'Closer' on *The Downward Spiral*, the means of getting closer to God are abusive heterosexual sex – violent feeling gets you closer to God. This would be inappropriate for Doe, who seems to have no (or possibly homo) sexuality. Yet the idea that you can get closer to something you might call God through self-willed, intense violence could explain Doe's final feeling of beatitude. The film itself does not endorse or believe in this religiosity either, but there is a mesmerising beauty to the Nine Inch Nails track, especially in co-ordination with the imagery of the credits, a co-ordination that evokes the fascination of the US underground and its self-proclaimed doer of evil, Kenneth Anger. Just as the pull of Renaissance sin literature is felt by the film, so is the appeal of this crypto-Satanism.

However, religion, Christian and otherwise, does not in the end provide salvation or transcendent explanation for us (as opposed to Doe), even if the grandeur of its vision is fully acknowledged. A second possible source of these, closely related to religion, is culture.

When I mentioned *Seven* to Marina Vitale, then Professor of English at the University of Salerno, she said, 'Of course I love that – it's so intellectual.' Her 'of course' was rueful about herself and the film, acknowledging the degree to which it wears its learning on its sleeve. This is evident in the scattering of high cultural references, including the religious texts (more famous as literature than theology), Bach and Shakespeare (*The Merchant of Venice*, quoted by Doe by having Gould, the Greed victim, cut off a pound of his own flesh), as well as middlebrow writing (*Of Human Bondage*, *In Cold Blood*), modernism (the Marquis de Sade, Thelonious Monk and Charlie Parker, the US underground, Andy Warhol's Campbell's Soup tins)[47] and post-modernism (Nine Inch Nails, David Bowie, performance art).

While we don't need to know any of these references to follow the film, we are invited into a complex relation to those who don't, represented by Mills. On the one hand, he is Brad Pitt – an audience is as likely to relate to his unfamiliarity with high culture as to feel superior to him; US student audiences identify and laugh about the all too familiar black-and-yellow covers of Cliff's *Pass Notes* before the close-up that lets anyone unfamiliar with them know what they are. Yet this already presupposes at least a college education, some accumulation of cultural capital. At other moments you have to know more than Mills to get the joke. When he mispronounces de Sade, it's only funny if you know who the singer Sade is, while we need to know that *Of Human Bondage* is not an s/m tract, as Somerset presumes Mills presumes. This places the film itself on the side of high culture, something perhaps

The underground look of *Seven*'s credits

referenced, Bignell suggests,[48] in showing the translation of Dante by Dorothy L. Sayers, who was also a celebrated crime novelist, and thus a precedent for the compatibility of high culture and the thriller genre. This is then borne out by other aspects of *Seven* that classify it as tantamount to an art movie: the perfect abstraction of its structures (more important than the more immediate pleasures of mystery and suspense supplied along the way), the fact that you can't see or hear it according to the norms of mainstream cinema, the beauty of its glimpsed cadavers, the bleakness of its ending. This is, as Vitale rightly implied, just the kind of thing intellectuals like.

Seven addresses us as people familiar with high culture and in its bleakness provides us with the complacent consolation of pessimism. Intellectuals and artists are brought up to have an enhanced understanding of life with next to no influence on it; bleakness provides us with the solace that the world is in any case irremediable and at least we can see that it is; bleakness is knowing better, a consolation for impotence. The high cultural reverberations of *Seven* situate it within this attitude and give a respectability, lineage and elaboration quite different from the grubbiness of, say, *Maniac* or the strained affirmation of *The Silence of the Lambs*.

To this we may add that the formal perfection of the film is a miraculous production of beauty out of ugliness and despair. But then this is also what Doe himself achieves through his perfect sequence of murders. The consolation of art's perfection in a desperately imperfect world is often lined with such sinister implications.

Religion and culture provide the grandeur of a perception of sin and despair, and there is a funny kind of consolation in this, but neither provides hope, salvation or cure. We are left with the more modest possibilities of human goodness.

One manifestation of this is humour. The sense that this at least allows one to make the best of a bad job, to get you through the day, is evoked by the film. The gallows humour common in professions cleaning up after human wreckage (medicine, policing, psychiatry) is evident in many comic lines: Somerset's dry 'Thank you, Doctor,' after the latter has pronounced the glaringly obvious diagnosis that the Fat Boy is dead; Mills's riff early on to the police captain, when Somerset says he doesn't want the case and Mills is too inexperienced for it: 'Give it to me. He doesn't want it. Fuck him. Sorry, but, see you later, have a nice time. Give it to me'; Doe's flat protestation of innocence, when a dead dog is found at the final murder scene: 'I didn't do that.'

In principle these do provide some sort of resort in the presence of horror, but they don't add up to a representation of the healing power of laughter. First, Doe is as ironically witty as Somerset is dry. Secondly, Mills's humour is signalled as part of aural pollution (see Chapter 5, 'Sound'). Thirdly, the key moment of humour seems to me not to work. This is at the Mills's apartment. After dinner, a subway train clatters by, causing the dinner table things to rattle and the record player to jump. Mills expresses his exasperation that the estate agent only brought them there for short periods at a time so they had not known what they were in for. There is a pause, then Somerset says ruminatively, 'The soothing, relaxing, vibrating home' and laughs, the others joining in, Tracy wholeheartedly, Mills less so. This is a standard feelgood moment in American movies and television of the past twenty years, the dissolution of conflict and tension in the community of laughter. Here in *Seven* (as very often) it seems to me quite fake. I find myself wanting to raise the pernickety realist objection that if it were only possible to visit the house for short periods, how come they've now sat through a long meal without it happening? This detail of faltering realism in a film so careful to keep its realist co-ordinates in place (even while producing so stylised an overall effect) seems to me to suggest a lack of conviction about such bonding through humour.

Which leaves us with the two good people: Tracy and Somerset. They are connected, not only by a shared taste for African-American music but also in Tracy's discussion with Somerset about what to do about being pregnant. It is not just that she hasn't told Mills and feels more able to talk to Somerset (whom she hardly knows), but that, it turns out, he has faced the same dilemma. He had a relationship with a woman, she became pregnant and Somerset was faced with the fear of bringing a child into a world like this.

It's significant that this is a matter of home and family. The dinner at the Mills's is one of the few nice, warm moments in the film. In an opening cut from the final version, Somerset visits a house that he thinks of buying for his retirement, a wooden house in a leafy area, an icon of the American dream. There is at first no sound at all, and then when he goes outside, only the song of birds and a light ambient background. He remarks to the agent that it seems strange; oh no, the latter assures him, there's nothing strange here. 'That's what I mean,' says Somerset. It all symbolises a normality utterly absent from the city, but also from the film as we now have it, where it is not even present as an ideal or possibility. Somerset cuts a piece of wallpaper from the house and, in some shots necessarily cut from the scene at the Mills's, it falls from his wallet; Tracy asks him what it is and he says, 'My future'. She at once understands and also comments on how nice it is to see a man being tender about such things ('David would say [a man like that] was a fag'). The moment reinforced the relation between Tracy and Somerset, one founded on the values of domesticity.

With such references to the home as have been omitted from the film, we are left only with Tracy to embody this possibility. Many are impressed by Gwyneth Paltrow's performance in the role and she is sometimes lit with the characteristic angelic glow of (white) women stars. Yet for all that she is a thinly realised character. She is in the film very little and exists as a function of the plot, of Mills's tragic destiny, and as a series of traces (see Chapter 3, 'Structure') that signal her importance to him. She is a fragile representation of the hope of love and family, and then even this hope is snuffed out by the terrible revelation of her death. This last seems to me, *toutes proportions guardées*, comparable to the death of Cordelia in *King Lear*. Another embodiment of goodness, also rather underdeveloped in the writing, who, just when you expect deliverance, is announced dead. Both cases are devastating for what they mean, but this is located in the man's suffering and his loss of a male fantasy of domestic repose.

It is significant that Somerset's joke ('the vibrating home') is gently at the expense of this ideal. In the film now he has no refuge, his home is

anonymous and orderly (or just 'masculine'?) and he has deliberately
chosen celibacy and childlessness. Somerset's is not a heroic, idealised
goodness but one fusing small signs of concern and respect with a gentle,
calm approach to the world. He cares ('Did the kid see it?'), he has pity
(rejecting Mills's attitude to the Gluttony victim – 'How'd the fat fuck
even fit out his front door?', 'Please – it's obvious he'd been shut in'), he
is able to sympathise, as Tracy intuits. Against the overwhelming force of
sin, he is doing the best he can, not shrugging his shoulders like the
captain ('it's the way it's always been') or the sex club owner ('that's life,
isn't it?'), setting his metronome to provide some sense of orderliness in
a world wholly lacking in it.

 Yet even that sense of doing what one can in a small way in one's
little neck of the woods he glosses despairingly. He tells Mills (who, no
doubt genuinely, mouths the rhetoric of 'I thought I could do some good'
within minutes of their meeting) that he sees their job as 'picking up the
pieces in case we get lucky'. And he smashes the metronome, as if in
acknowledgment that one cannot keep the noise and darkness at bay.
The moment is as symbolically forceful as Tracy's death, since it
extinguishes even this frail beacon of goodness in a naughty world.

 In the final car journey, the editing dissociates Somerset from Mills
and Doe; they are behind bars, he is not (see Chapter 3, 'Structure').
Doe takes the logic of the notion of sin to its conclusion: if we are all
drenched in sin, then so is he. Yet somehow, inconsistently, Somerset

Tracy tells Somerset she is pregnant

remains outside of this, without sin. The film relies, with excellent judgement, on Morgan Freeman to carry off this contradiction: his repose, the expressivity we see in his eyes, the mellow timbre of his voice give Somerset an unforgettable presence. All qualities of performance enact ways of being in the world. These, of Freeman as Somerset, are passive, not exerting pressure on self or the world, not implicated or involved. Somerset can be separated from Mills and Doe, from sin, only at the cost of not participating in the world. And the proof of this is that he fails to save Mills. The good can only look on and despair.

Seven ends with Somerset's voice saying over a dirty yellow gathering gloom, 'Ernest Hemingway once wrote, "the world is a fine place and worth fighting for." I agree with the second part.' It was a cap desired by the studio,[49] intended to give some crumb of Hollywoodian comfort in a film so extraordinarily un-American in its pessimism. It works as a futile pronouncement. It is at once engulfed, first in the return to the darkness with which the film opens and the aural pollution (here helicopter blades) that never leaves it, then with the scratched

credits, evoking both Doe and the police, and the bitterness of 'The Hearts Filthy Lesson' with its despairingly apocalyptic refrain, 'If there was only some kind of future.' But even without this engulfment, the cap would provide no succour.

'You know, this isn't going to have a happy ending.'

It makes me think again of *King Lear*. At the very end of the play, in a world wrenched apart, human iniquity triumphant, the character of Edgar brings things to a close with the following:

The weight of this sad time we must obey;
Speak what we feel, not what we ought to say.
The oldest hath borne most: we that are young
Shall never see so much, nor live so long.

It is a pronouncement at once opaque and banal and can scarcely constitute an adequate suturing of the wounds the play has opened up with such monumental ferocity. Neither can Somerset's in *Seven*. Both are gestures at salvation which nothing before them gives any warrant for. They are – in both the dismissive and profound sense of the word – pathetic.

In *Seven* there is neither 'health in us' nor divine mercy. The film is a single-minded elaboration on a feeling that the world is beyond both redemption and remedy. In life this feeling may be – perhaps has to be – passing, but it is the province of art to isolate, focus, refine and exaggerate feelings. The affective keynote of *Seven* is darkness – of sound as well as sight – and any lightness only serves to bring out the unyielding character of that darkness. It is a gripping story, but even more it is a landscape of despair, a symphony of sin.

If Somerset had shot John Doe, according to the films theme John Does act would be stripped of his intended-desired meaning by Somersets 'Self-sacrifice' but Somerset demands impossible 'sacrifice' from David. Somersets complicity with John Doe's crime

Notes

1 See Geoffrey Ashe, *The Ancient Wisdom* (London: Macmillan, 1977) for further elaboration of the prevalence of the heptad (i.e. groups of seven).

2 Maria Matzer, 'Selling Seven', *Hollywood Reporter* vol. 342 no. 42, 18 June 1996, pp. S13–S15.

3 I'm grateful to Ian Garwood and Sissel Vik for discussing both this and the final 'Hearts Filthy Lesson' tracks with me.

4 Rape and paedophilia are sins of lust, but it is not for them that Doe kills, respectively, Eli Gould (Greed) and Victor (Sloth).

5 Following the film's own practice, I refer to Tracy by her first name but the two detectives by their last. Tracy makes a point about this, when Somerset comes to dinner, introducing 'William' and 'David' to one another. Much later in the film, drinking together in a bar after the 'Lust' murder, Mills says good–bye, saying 'Thank you, Bill,' signalling the closeness they have reached.

6 Mark Salisbury, 'Seventh Hell', *Empire* vol. 80, February 1996, pp. 78–87.

7 On the soundtrack commentary to the Criterion Collection laserdisc.

8 Scott Reynolds, 'Taking Chances', *Sight and Sound* vol. 8 no. 2, NS, February 1998, p. 61

9 For a discussion, see Christopher Ames, 'Restoring the Black Man's Lethal Weapon', *Journal of Popular Film and Television* vol. 20 no. 3, Fall 1992, pp. 53–60.

10 Veljohnson only appears briefly in *Die Hard 2*; Jackson appears only in the third film, and as a crime-busting partner but not a cop.

11 'Killer Movie', *Film Review*, February 1996, pp. 33–42. (Interview with David Fincher by Judy Sloane, pp. 34–5.)

12 Neither did Fincher when he read the script. See Vachaud, Laurent, 'Entretien avec David Fincher: Dans les cercles

de l'Enfer', *Positif* vol. 420, 1996, pp. 83–6, p. 85.

13 In Salisbury, 'Seventh Hell', pp. 78–87.

14 Cf. Deborah Cameron, and Elizabeth Frazer, *The Lust to Kill* (London: Polity, 1987); Denis Dudos, *The Werewolf Complex: America's Fascination with Violence* (Oxford: Berg, 1998); Richard Dyer, 'Kill and Kill Again', *Sight and Sound* vol. 7 no. 9, NS, 1997, pp. 14–17; Philip Jenkins, *Using Murder: The Social Construction of Serial Homicide* (New York: Aldine de Gruyter, 1994); Richard Tithecott, *Of Men and Monsters: Jeffrey Dahmer and the Construction of the Serial Killer* (Madison: University of Wisconsin Press, 1997); Judith Walkowitz, *City of Dreadful Delight* (Chicago: University of Chicago Press, 1992), Chapter 7 and epilogue.

15 Kemper was convicted of eight murders in 1973 (six young women, his mother and her best friend); he had also killed his grandparents when he was fifteen.

16 Bond was a forensic pathologist who carried out post–mortems on two of the Ripper victims. His report is reprinted in Donald Rumbelow, *The Complete Jack the Ripper* (London: Penguin, 1988), pp. 130–41.

17 Walkowitz, *City*, p. 196.

18 A note for those worrying about my arithmetic. Doe does not kill Mills (who is within the sins chain), but does kill Tracy (who isn't). By kill in this context I include cause to be killed – Doe himself only directly kills Sloth and Tracy; he gets Gluttony, Greed and Pride to kill themselves and someone else to kill Lust and Envy (i.e. himself). Wrath (Mills) he gets to destroy himself, though not literally to kill himself.

19 Royal S. Brown, 'Seven', *Cineaste* vol. XII no. 3, 1996, pp. 44–6.

20 José Arroyo, 'Brad Pitt – the Making of a

Super Icon', *Attitude*, December 1997, pp. 68–74.

21 David Lloyd, 'Race under Representation', *Oxford Literary Review*, vol. 13 nos. 1–2, 1991, pp. 62–94; Richard Dyer, *White* (London: Routledge, 1997).

22 'Three Questions about Serial Killing', *First of the Month* vol. 1, 1998, pp. 18–19.

23 Cf. Lucy Bland, 'The Case of the Yorkshire Ripper: Mad, Bad, Beast or Male?' in Jill Radford and Diane E. H. Russell, (eds), *Femicide: The Politics of Women Killing* (Buckingham: Open University Press, 1992), pp. 233–52.

24 Found guilty in 1892 of murdering four prostitutes in London; in a study of him, Angus McLaren observes that such a serial killer is 'likely best understood not so much as an "outlaw" as an "oversocialized" individual who saw himself simply carrying out sentences that society at large levelled' (i.e. against prostitutes) (Angus McLaren, *A Prescription for Murder: The Victorian Serial Killings of Dr. Thomas Neill Cream* (Chicago: University of Chicago Press, 1993), p. xiii; quoted in Mark Selzer, *Serial Killers* (London: Routledge, 1998), p. 44).

25 Cf. Caputi, *Age of the Sex Crime*; Wendy Holloway, ''I Just Wanted to Kill a Woman." Why? The Ripper and Male Sexuality', *Feminist Review* vol. 9, 1981, pp. 33–40; Cameron and Frazer, *The Lust To Kill*; Radford and Russell, *Femicide*; Walkowitz, *City*, pp. 229–45.

26 Andrea Dworkin, *Pornography: Men Possessing Women* (New York: Perigree, 1981), p.53.

27 First published in *Weird Tales*, July 1943; reprinted in Lester Del Rey (ed.), *The Best of Robert Bloch* (New York: Ballantine, 1977).

28 *Screen International* vol. 1041, 9 January 1996, p. 8.

29 Fincher: 'We trimmed stuff for Morgan. Morgan is one of those guys who'll come up to you and go, "I can just look at the guy and do all this, you can cut this stuff"' (Sloane, 'Killer Movie', p. 34).

30 Identified as such by Gould's widow; behind it are the words 'Help me' written by Victor's hand.

31 Kerry Anne Burrows, 'Inside Darius Khondji', *Eyepiece* vol. 17 no. 5, 1996, pp. 23–7.

32 E.g. Pete Boss, 'Vile Bodies and Bad Medicine', *Screen* vol. 27, 1986, pp. 14–24; Barbara Creed, *The Monstrous–Feminine: Film, Feminism, Psycho–analysis* (New York: Routledge, 1993); Isabel Cristina Pinedo, *Recreational Terror: Women and the Pleasures of Horror Film Viewing* (Albany: SUNY Press, 1997).

33 Cf. the discussion of geography and invisibility in *The Silence of the Lambs* in Norman Gobetti, *Jonathan Demme: Il silenzio degli innocenti* (Turin: Lindau, 1997).

34 For a discussion of this see Tithecott, *Men and Monsters,* pp.105–8 and Dyer, 'Three Questions'.

35 Pinedo, *Recreational Terror*.

36 Burrows, 'Inside Darius Khondji', p. 25.

37 Chris Darke, 'Inside the Light', *Sight and Sound* vol. 6 no. 4, NS, 1996, pp. 18–20, p. 20.

38 David E. Williams, 'The Sins of a Serial Killer', *American Cinematographer* vol. 76 no. 10, 1995, pp. 34–42.

39 Ibid., p. 37.

40 Salisbury, 'Seventh Hell', p. 87.

41 Sloane, 'Killer Movie', p. 35.

42 Criterion Collection laserdisc.

43 All references to Khondji in this paragraph are from Williams, 'Sins of a Serial Killer'.

44 Darke, 'Inside the Light', p. 20.

45 *Radio Times,* 12–18 September 1998, pp. 44–5.

46 Jonathan Bignell, 'The Detective at the End of History: Postmodern Apocalypse in *The Name of the Rose* and *Seven*', in *Postmodern Media Culture: Theoretical Discourses and Their Objects* (Edinburgh: Edinburgh University Press, forthcoming).

47 Ibid.

48 Ibid.

49 Morgan Freeman on Criterion Laserdisc.

Credits

Se7en

USA 1995

Director
David Fincher
Producers
Arnold Kopelson, Phyllis
Carlyle
Screenplay
Andrew Kevin Walker
Director of Photography
Darius Khondji
Edited by
Richard Francis-Bruce
Production Design
Arthur Max
Music
Howard Shore

©New Line Productions. Inc
Production Company
New Line Cinema presents
an Arnold Kopelson
production
a film by David Fincher
Executive Producers
Gianni Nunnari, Dan
Kolsrud, Anne Kopelson
Co-executive Producers
Lynn Harris, Richard
Saperstein
Additional Photography
Line Producer
William C. Gerrity
Co-producers
Stephen Brown, Nana
Greenwald, Sanford Panitch
Associate Producer
Michele Platt

**Executive in Charge of
Production**
Ted Zachary
**Supervising Production
Executive**
Carla Fry
Production Controller
Paul Prokop
Production Co-ordinator
Wendy Cox
**In-house Production
Co-ordinator**
Emily Glatter
**Assistant Production
Co-ordinator**
John L. Anderson
Unit Production Managers
Allan Wertheim, Robert S.
Mendelsohn
Location Managers
Paul Hargrave
Additional Photography:
Flint Maloney
**Assistant Location
Manager**
Flint Maloney
Location Assistant
Joseph Johnston Jr
Location Scouts
Richard Schuler
Additional Photography:
Rick Schnier
**Executive in Charge of
Post-production**
Joe Finman
**Post-production
Supervisor**
Ric Keeley
**Post-production
Co-ordinator**
Mark Graziano

Post-production PA
Ian Crockett
Production Accountant
Robert J. Grindrod
1st Assistant Accountant
Jerri Whiteman
Payroll Accountant
Brad Davis
**Additional Photography
Accountant**
Fred Grossman
Accounting Assistant
Hedi El Kholti
Construction Estimator
Roxanne Reaver
Business Affairs Liaisons
Ginny Martino, Liz Amsden
Production Attorneys
Phillip Rosen, Avy
Eschenasy
Production Secretary
Janet Stirner
Office Staff Assistants
Basil Grillo, Anna Rita
Nunnari Dell'Atte
Additional Photography:
Michael Cutler
Set Production Assistants
Adam M. Stone, Kenneth
Frith
Assistant to Mr Kopelson
Maria Norman
Assistant to Mr Fincher
Rachel Schadt
Assistant to Mr Freeman
Quentin Pierre
1st Assistant Directors
Nilo Otero, Michael Alan
Kahn
2nd Assistant Director
Frank Davis

Additional Photography
Key 2nd Assistant
Directors
Scott Harris, George
Fortmuller
2nd 2nd Assistant
Directors
Dodi Rubenstein, Craig
Pinckes
Additional Photography:
Rebecca Strickland
Additional 2nd Assistant
Directors
Leonard M. Bram, David
Ticotin
DGA Trainee
Tyrone Walker
Script Supervisors
Cori Glazer
Additional Photography
Additional:
Jane Goldsmith
Casting
Billy Hopkins, Suzanne
Smith, Kerry Borden
Casting Associate
Aisha Coley
LA Casting Assistant
Kim Coleman
NY Casting Assistant
Jennifer McNamara
Extras Casting
Central Casting
Additional Photography
Aerial Cameraman
Don Morgan
A Camera Operator
Conrad W. Hall
Additional Photography
Camera Operator
Jeff Cronenweth

B Camera Operators
Michael Chavez
Additional Photography:
Mitch Dubin
1st Assistant Camera
Brad Edmiston
Additional Photography:
Julian Whatley
2nd Assistant Camera
Paul Prince
Additional Photography:
Steve Matzinger
Camera Loader
David Sanchez
Additional Photography B
Camera 1st Assistant
Greg Schmidt
Additional Photography B
Camera 2nd Assistant
Brent Beal
Steadicam Operator
David Emmerichs
Steadicam Assistant
Dale Myrand
Additional Photography
Gyrosphere Operator
Michael Kelem
Additional Photography
Wescam Operator
Stan McClain
Additional Photography
Wescam Technician
Michael Charbonnet
Special Colour
Consultant
Yvon Lucas
Stills Photographer
Peter Sorel
John Doe's Photographs
Melodie McDaniel

Key Grips
Michael Coo
Additional Photography:
Mike Popovich
Best Boy Grips
William E. Fitch
Additional Photography:
Tom Gibson
Dolly Grips
Michael Brennan
Additional Photography:
Mark Myers
Additional Photography
2nd:
Tommy Ruffner
Grips
Nico Bally, Daniel Cook, Billy
Bob Leslie
Key Rigging Grip
Larry Aube
Rigging Grips
Dennis McLean, John
McGraham, Anthony Petrilla
Chief Lighting Technician
Chris Strong
Additional Photography
Gaffer
Claudio Miranda
Additional Photography
Best Boy Gaffer
Eddie Maloney
Electrics Co-ordinator
Peter Davidian
Electricians
William Travis McKane, Jeff
Strong, Monty Woodard,
Mike Bonnaud, Adam Glick,
Ed Medin, Chris Franco
Additional Photography
Electrics
Mike Adler, Shawn Goldstein

Video Engineer
Tom 'Chick Magnet' Loewy
Video Equipment
Video Hawks
**Digital Visual
Effects/Computer
Generated Imagery**
R/Greenberg Associates
West, Inc
**Visual Effects/Main Title
Producers**
Peter Frankfurt, Steven T.
Puri
Visual Effects Supervisor
Greg Kimble
**Visual Effects
Co-ordinator**
Tim Thompson
**Special Effects
Co-ordinator**
Peter Albiez
**Special Effects
Supervisor**
Danny Cangemi
Special Effects
William B. Doane, Robert A.
Phillips, Eric Dresser,
Lambert Powell, Rich Ratliff,
Whitey Crumb
Seven Graphic Displays
Video Image, Paul
Taglianetti, Demian
Rosenblatt, Pete Martinez
Editor
William Hoy
1st Assistant Editor
Robert Charles Lusted
2nd Assistant Editor
Howard Davis
Assistant Editors
Lindsay Mofford, Laura P.

Krasnow, Carol Folgate, Tom
Barrett
Avid Assistant
David Reale
Art Directors
Gary Wissner
Additional Photography:
Vincent Reynaud
Assistant Art Director
Barry Chusid
Set Designers
Elizabeth Lapp, Lori
Rowbathom, Hugo Santiago
Illustrators
Patrick Tatopoulos, Thomas
Lay, Sean Hargreaves,
Daren Dochterman
Storyboard Artist
Jacques Rey
**Art Department
Co-ordinator**
Jan O'Connell
Set Decorator
Clay A. Griffith
Lead Man
Chris Gibbin
Assistant Set Decorator
Brana Michelle Rosenfeld
On Set Dresser
John H. Maxwell
Set Decorating Buyer
Elizabeth Ragagli
Swing Gang
Gregory J. Wilkinson, James
Bowen Jr, Chris Pascuzzo,
Bruce Bellamy
Draper
Erich Baumann
**Construction
Co-ordinators**
Robert Bonino

Additional Photography:
Daniel Ray Pemberton
**Assistant Construction
Co-ordinator**
Todd A. Young
Construction Foremen
Edward H. Wouters, William
Roscoe Davidson, Todd
McKibben, Brian J. Geary
Paint Foreman
Gerald J. Gates
Paint Assistant Foreman
Maureen Kropf
Plaster Foreman
Michael Sanchez
Labour Foremen
Thomas Sahli, Kelly Birrer,
D. Ray Reid
**Painter Decorator Gang
Bosses**
Antonio Santelli, Charles
Lungren, Michael Mikita Jr,
Michael Mikita Sr, Mitchell
Simmons
Labour Gang Bosses
Van Jewell, Eric Sherman
Plasters
Salvador Sanchez, Ernest
Quintero, Leo Mouneau Sr,
David Rodriguez
Painter Decorators
Shawn Albro, Tim Stadler,
Jay Schmiddt, Russel
Harvey, Joanne Davis,
Rafael Lopez, Jon Maaso,
Ed Cornell, Daren Cornell,
Monty McCrae, William
Walrner
Labour HOD
Eli Jimenez

Labour Toolroom Keepers
Virgil Ross, David A. Bonino
Labourers
Jesse Rosenfeld, Thayne
Scott Reos, James
Donohue, Armand
Gonzalez, Alad Safdeye,
Robert Rodriguez, Edward
Alvarado Jr, Robert Flores,
Stuart Gates, Leopold
Mouneau Jr, Mitchell
Thompson, Robert
Schmeck, Bill Scholl
Graffiti Artist
Ernest Vales
Stand-by Painter
Nicholas C. John
Props Master
Roy 'Bucky' Moore
Prop Assistant
Mike Cunningham
Propmaker Gang Bosses
Dale Saiger, Earl Betts, Joe
Valentino, Michael S. O'Neal,
Donald Redoglia
Propmakers
Denny L. White, Roger
Reeco, Jay Harris, Don
Yaklin, Devlin Lerew, Michael
Sullivan, John Bistagne,
Joseph Gilmore, Alan
Alvarado, Kevin McCown,
Richard Wheeler, Richard E.
Ross, Raull Butcher, David
Reyes, Joseph J Lagoia,
Phillip A. Henry, Heinz
Strunk, Barry Berrison,
Robbie Watts, Gregory
Hamlin, Alex Temme, Caleb
Harris, George Harris,
George Stewart, Nicholas

Stewart, Thomas Early,
Sasha Madzar, Laszlo
Veszpeller, Earl Forkrud,
Dale Hart
Costume Designer
Michael Kaplan
Costume Supervisor
Elinor C. Bardach
Costumers
Marsha Bozeman, Lawrence
Velasco
Make-up Supervisor
Jean Black
**Mr Freeman's Make-up
Artist**
Michael A Hancock
**Supervising Hair/Make-up
Artist**
Michael White
Make-up Artist
Monty Westmore
Special Make-up Effects
Rob Bottin
**Rob Bottin Production
Crew**
Effects Producer:
Fernando Favila
Project Co-ordinator:
Dawn Severdia
Sculptor.
Motoyoshi Hata
Model/Moldmaker:
Art Pinemtel
Conceptual Artist:
James Feldman
Make-up Artist:
Margaret Prentice
Hair Design:
Becky Ochoa
Painter:
Thomas Floutz

Effects Photographer:
Anette Haellmigk
Key Artists:
Linda Frobos, Todd Weslow,
Ryan Peterson, Robin
McDonald, Dave Smith, Jack
Bricker, Anthony Barlow,
Greg Solomon, Sam Sainz,
Eva Marie Denst
Main/End Titles
Design/Exccution
Kyle Cooper
Main Title Opticals
Pacific Title
Opticals
Cinema Research
**Special Image
Manipulation**
Findlay Bunting
Colour Timer
Dale Caldwell
Score Conductor
Lucas Richman
Orchestrations
Bert Dovo, John Lissauer
**Computer Music
Programming**
Simon Franglen
**Executive in Charge of
Music**
Toby Emmerich
Music Executive
Dana Sano
Music Co-ordinator
Mark Kaufman
Music Contractor
Sandy DeCrescent
Music Preparation
Janice Hayen
Assistant to Mr Shore
Robert C. Cotnoir

Music Editors
Ellen Segal, Angie Rubin
Music Consultants for Mr Fincher
Rachel Schadt, Ren Klyce
Music Scoring Mixer
John Kurlander
Mixing Engineer
John Richards
Soundtrack
"Closer" by Trent Reznor, performed by Nine Inch Nails; "El Michoacano" by Demetrio Farias, performed by El Mariachi Tepalcatepec; "Suite No. 3 in D Major" by Johann Sebastian Bach, perfomed by Stuttgart Chamber Orchestra, conducted by Karl Muchinger; "Trouble Man" by/performed by Marvin Gaye; "Straight, No Chaser" by/performed by Thelonius Monk; "Now's the Time" by/performed by Charlie Parker; "Love Plus One" by Nick Hayward, performed by Haircut 100; "I Cover the Waterfront" by John W. Green, Edward Heyman, performed by Billie Holiday; "Lust" by/performed by Ren Klyce, Steve Boeddeker; "In the Beginning" by Doris Cochran, Kay Twomey, Ben Weisman, Fred Wise, performed by The Statler Brothers; "Guilty" by Bill Leeb, Rhys Fulber, performed by Front Line

Assembly; " Speaking of Happiness" by Jimmy Radcliffe, Buddy Scott, performed by Gloria Lynne; "The Hearts Filthy Lesson" by David Bowie, Brian Eno, Reeves Gabrels, Mike Garson, Erdal Kizilcay, Sterling Campbell, performed by David Bowie; "Gypsy Csardas"; "The Fourth Man"
Sound Designer/Effects Supervisor
Ren Klyce
Assistant Sound Supervisor
Yin Cantor
Production Sound Mixer
Willie D. Burton
Recordists
Jack Keller, David Behle
Re-recording Mixers
Robert J. Litt, Rick Hart, Elliot Tyson
Supervising Sound Editor
Patrick Dodd
Dialogue Editors
John Nutt, Francesca Dodd
Assistant Dialogue Editor
Erik Kraber
Sound Effects Editors
Kim B. Christensen, Jennifer Ware
Assistant Sound Effects Editors
Steve Boeddeker, Jeffrey Kroeber, Sean Callery, Nancy Jencks

Apprentice Sound Effects Editors
Chris Halstead, Sarah Felpes
Boom Operator
Marvin E. Lewis
Utility Sound Technician
Robert W. Harris
Conforming Editor
Rich Quinn
Negative Cutting
Kona Cutting, Gary Burritt
Foley Artists
Margie O'Malley, Marnie Moore
Foley Mixers
Richard Duarte, Jeremy Molad
Foley Editor
Malcolm Fife
ADR Supervisor
Patrick Dodd
ADR Recordist
Rick Canelli
ADR Mixer
Thomas J. O'Connell
ADR Editors
Jeff Watts, Joan Chapman, Mark Levinson
Police Advisers
Call the Cops, Randy Walker, Mark Arneson, Ed Arneson
Medical Consultant
Dr Robert M. Rey, MD
Stunt Co-ordinator/ Additional Photography Stunt Co-ordinator
Charles Picerni Jr
Stunts
Sandy Berumen, Johny Martin, Lafaye Baker, Janet

Brady, Bob Brown, Charles
Picerni Jr, Cindy Daniels,
Kane Hodder, Henry Kingi,
Alan Oliney, Steve Picerni,
Tim Davison, Gary Price,
Kenny Endoso, Pat Romano,
Andre Gibbs, Phillip J.
Romano, Scott Wilder, Bill
Young's Precision Driving
Team
Additional Photography
Precision Driver
Co-ordinator
Dennis Alpert
Brad Pitt's Double
Richie Varga
Kevin Spacey's Double
Patrick Barnett
Brad Pitt's Stand-in
Thomas Brader
Morgan Freeman's
Stand-in
Bob Collins
Additional Photography
Aerial Co-ordinator
Chuck Tamburro
Preview Technical
Supervisor
Lee Tucker
Animals Supplied
Studio Animal Service
Animal Trainer
Paul Calabria
Unit Publicist
Susan Steinlauf
International Public
Relations
Dennis Davidson Associates
Copyright Clearances
Clearvision, Lana Hale

Product Placement
Tony Hoffman
First Aid
Jeffrey Stevens
Additional Photography:
Alex Barnoya
Transportation
Co-ordinators
Russell McEntyre
Additional Photography:
Al Kaminsky
Transportation Captain
Wayne Stone
Drivers
Bonnie Alden, Michael R.
McEntyre, George Alden,
Alan Myers, Alex Algozzino,
Jerry A. Oliveri, Joseph
Campise, Sergio Orosco,
Patrick J. Elmendorf, Scott
Pierson, Bo Falck, Dewey A.
Reed, Robert A. Gaskill,
Keith Stearns, Jeff J. Hattem,
Steve Surabian, Gary J.
Johnson, Randy L.
Thiederman, Al Kaminsky,
Gaston Touchard, Bob
Limon, Raymond Van
Holten, Juan Lopez, Tom
Whelpley, James A. Lundin,
Robert T. White, Larry
Market, Emmett L. Willis,
Michael W. McClure, Eddie
Wirth, Brian McEntyre, Tony
Zahn, Jim McEntyre
Craft Service
Ron Hairston
Additional Photography:
Buz Kramer
Soup Lady
Suzanne Steptoe

Caterer
Michelson's Food Service
Chef
Jose Mojica
Sous Chefs
Marco Mojica, Benjamin
Padilla

Brad Pitt
Detective David Mills
Morgan Freeman
Detective William Somerset
Gwyneth Paltrow
Tracy Mills
Richard Roundtree
Talbot
R. Lee Ermey
police captain
John C. McGinley
California
Julie Araskog
Mrs Gould
Mark Boone Junior
greasy FBI man
John Cassini
Officer Davis
Reynald E. Cathey
Dr Santiago
Peter Crombie
Dr O'Neill
Hawthorne James
George the night guard at
the library
Michael Massee
man in booth at massage
parlour
Leland Orser
crazed man in massage
parlour
Richard Portnow
Dr Beardsley

Richard Schiff
Mark Swarr
Pamala Tyson
thin vagrant by John Doe's
apartment
Kevin Spacey
John Doe
Andy Walker
dead man at 1st crime
scene
Daniel Zacapa
Detective Taylor at first
murder
Bob Mack
gluttony victim
George Christy
workman at door of
Somerset's office
Endre Hules
cab driver
Roscoe Davidson
first guard at the library
Bob Collins
second guard at the library
Jimmy Dale Hartsell
library janitor
Charline Su
Dominique Jennings
TV news reporters
Allan Kolman
1st forensic man in the law
office
Beverly Burke
TV anchor woman
Gene Borkan
Eli Gould, sin of greed
Mario Di Donato
fingerprint forensic man in
law office
Alfonso Freeman
fingerprint technician

Harrison White
Robert Stephenson
cops on SWAT team
Michael Reid MacKay
Victor, sin of sloth
Tudor Sherrard
coupon man outside pizza
parlour
Lennie Loftin
policeman who takes
statement from vagrant
Sarah Hale Reinhardt
police sketch artist
Emily Wagner
Detective Sara at John Doe's
apartment
Martin Serene
Wild Bill
David Correia
1st cop at massage parlour
Ron Blair
2nd cop at massage parlour
Cat Mueller
hooker, sin of lust
Lexie Bigham
sweating cop at massage
parlour
Evan Miranda
Paul S. Eckstein
paramedics at massage
parlour
Harris Savides
pit operator
Rachel Schadt
additional pit operator
Heidi Schanz
beautiful woman, sin of pride
Brian Evers
duty sergeant
Shannon Wilcox
woman cop behind desk

Jim Deeth
John Santin
helicopter pilots
Charles Tamburro
SWAT helicopter pilot
Richmond Arquette
delivery man
Duffy Gaver
marksman in helicopter
Todd Potter
Purdy
Sexi Saudi
Mills's dogs

11,407 feet
127 minutes

Dolby/Digital DTS Sound
Colour by
DeLuxe Los Angeles
Prints by
DeLuxe Toronto
Super 35

Credits compiled by Markku
Salmi, BFI Filmographic Unit